THE
POWERS
OF
PRESENCE

D0208273

Robert Plant
Armstrong

THE
POWERS
OF
PRESENCE

CONSCIOUSNESS,
MYTH, AND
AFFECTING
PRESENCE

WITHDRAWN

University of Pennsylvania Press
Philadelphia
1981

Burgess

NB
1098
.A753

c. 2

The Author wishes to acknowledge the support of
The University of Texas at Dallas in the
preparation and publication of this work.

He further wishes to acknowledge support from
the following patrons:
—*Society of the Friends of African, Oceanic, and Indonesian
Art,* Suzanne Greub, Basel, Switzerland

—Mr. and Mrs. James H. W. Jacks

The lines from Voyages II are reprinted from *The
Complete Poems and Selected Letters and Prose of Hart Crane,*
edited by Brom Weber, and are used with the
permission of Liveright Publishing Corporation.
Copyright 1933, © 1958, 1966 by Liveright
Publishing Corporation.

Figure 2 is reprinted from page 47 of G. J. Afolabi
Ojo, *Yoruba Palaces: A Study of Afins of Yorubaland,*
University of London, 1966. Reprinted by
permission of Hodder & Stoughton Limited.

Copyright © 1981 by the University of
Pennsylvania Press.
All rights reserved.

Library of Congress Cataloging in Publication Data

Armstrong, Robert Plant.
  The powers of presence.

  Bibliography: p.
  Includes index.
  1. Sculpture, Primitive—Africa, West.
2. Sculpture, African—Africa, West. 3. Art and
anthropology. I. Title.
NB1098.A753   730'.0966   81–51136
ISBN 0–8122–7804–6   AACR2

Printed in the United States of America

1965 JAN 17   IW.

To
Earl W. Count
and
Henry H. Glassie

CONTENTS

PLATES

Selected by John A. Buxton

(Plates follow page 130)

FIGURES

INTRODUCTION

Further inquiry into the human nature of "art" is necessary not because there are insufficient books devoted to the understanding of art, but rather because I feel such address as has been made has been conducted without sufficient liberation from the tyrannies of ethnocentrism. Thus both philosophers and anthropologists have, in my view, veered in the direction of skewing into familiar contours works which in profound respects might quite possibly be very different from what such workers might have supposed. Further, I was persuaded that the understanding of what is a human imperative, which is what "art" is, is not entirely possible in such studies because they have tended to lose sight of its imperatival urgencies under the notion that it is but a polite election; and they have denied it its ineluctable and inalienable estate as subject by making it (or *trying* to make it) a mere substitute or proxy for subjectivity.

I pursue here two ideas I introduced earlier in *The Affecting Presence* and *Wellspring.* These are that the work of "art" is a presence, and that it abides in power. Here I work in the directions of revealing further the conditions of the work's subjectivity and of showing the varieties of its power as well as how it is that power abides in the work.

The relationship between those two books and this one is rather analogous to the relationships among Mahler's symphonies, concerning which someone has observed that altogether they comprise but one long work. Themes are repeated from one symphony to the other, but each time a theme is introduced it gains greater subtlety and richer development. Thus, although two of the themes I develop were introduced in the earlier books, here they are unfolded so that one might come to a fuller perception of them. Because much of what I have to write about is at base ineffable, it is best said when it is multifariously said. The understanding is, mercifully, not identical with language—else we should be terribly limited. Thus the images I employ are intended to inject the blood and brooding of poetry into the sinews of prose, for poetry transcends its medium's limitations. "Art," in short, is a state of being not at all coterminous with the possibilities of propositional prose.

Still, though this work will be enriched by the other two books, it will stand by itself. It is its own work. And it is lean rather than corpulent. Through a dozen drafts I have, I hope, made it wiry. I trust it will grow stronger in exercise with the reader's attentions.

I am pleased to enter a word about the illustrations in this book. The works of African sculpture one sees in book after book tend to be the same ones. Thus these pieces seem, through frequency of use, to have become "classics." They would appear to have come to comprise a canon; however, any such writ is but an invention of Western Europeans and Americans, and has no African reality. In the collections of both individuals and museums there are many fine pieces which have received scant attention. Accordingly, in order both to attack the notion of "masterpieces" and also to increase the inventory of published works—for reasons relating to the amelioration of visual boredom and to the increase of the richness of scholarly reference—I have decided to rely upon these classics as little as possible. I have adopted the expedient of turning to experts—to those who daily engage in the activities of collecting. Mr. John Buxton of Shango Galleries in Dallas has spearheaded this effort to locate fine and fresh alternatives to the "canonical" pieces. Mr. Michael Oliver and Mr. Bryce Holcomb, the former of his own and the latter of Pace Galleries, have also lent their discriminating energies to the nomination of works to be here included. I am indebted to these gentlemen, as indeed I am to those individuals and institutions who have permitted their pieces to be published here—most of them for the first time.

I am also indebted to Professors John Povey, the University of California at Los Angeles; David Wilson and Daniel J. Crowley, the University of California at Davis; Roy Sieber and the late Alan P. Merriam, Indiana University, Bloomington; and Robert Farris Thompson of Yale. Through their invitations to give seminars or through their discussions with me, these scholars have encouraged me to continue and extend my thinking. I must also thank Eileen Tollett, who has worked with me through most of the many drafts of this book; and her fellow graduate students Cynthia Giles,

Julian Riepe, Dee Mitchell, and David Wright, each of whom has engaged with me in good discourse. Professor Rainer Schulte has read the manuscript of this work, making useful observations and offering staunch friendship. Also from the University of Texas at Dallas, Alexander L. Clark, Vice-President for Academic Affairs, provided a grant which helped meet some of the expense of manuscript preparation. Dr. Susan Vogel of the Metropolitan Museum of Art has been of great help with some of the photographic illustrations. John McGuigan of the University of Pennsylvania Press is especially acknowledged for his strong interest in and support of this work.

Of especial significance to the thinking and writing of this book have been two men whose support for and interest in my work have been unflagging. I hope they will not be embarrassed by my wish to dedicate this work to them: Earl W. Count, Professor Emeritus of Anthropology at Hamilton College, and Henry H. Glassie, Professor of Folklore at the University of Pennsylvania. The former made me think deeply about the nature of man the myth-making animal, and the latter about man the objectifier.

THE
POWERS
OF
PRESENCE

1 THE POWERS OF INVOCATION, THE POWERS OF VIRTUOSITY

In all cultures certain things exist which, though they may appear to be but ordinary objects, yet are treated in ways quite different from the ways in which objects are usually treated.

Consider, for example, a wedge-shaped stone about two inches in length and no more than one and a quarter inches at its widest part. The casual observer may think it to be no more than a stone brought to its present shape by the natural processes of wearing away that time brings about. More sophisticated viewers will observe that it has been worked to such a shape. But whatever the case, it is unlikely that either observer will be prepared for the honors paid to such a stone in a Yoruba village in west central Nigeria, by a Shango priest, who will bow before it, clapping his hands and reciting praise poems to it. What is this thing? Is it a god? Is it a relic of some special merit? Does it own power? Is it a work of art? Perhaps to the questioner's great surprise, each of these questions may be answered affirmatively: the stone celt is in some respect or other of divinity, meritorious, powerful, and a work of art; or, more properly, it belongs to that order of phenomena of which what we call "works of art" are but a suborder.

Such things as the wedge have spatiotemporal existence; they eventuate from processes of their making. They are, in these respects, quite clearly objects. But at the same time, peoples' behavior toward them argues that they are something more. Further consider the instance of a drum at the court of the king (the Asantehene) of the Ashanti people of Ghana. The instrument is played as any drum might be, but at the same time it is deemed to be of a sexual specificity (some are male, others female), it is offered sacrifices, and poetry is also recited in its honor, the poetically established virtues somehow enriching the drum itself—as indeed do its sexuality and

3

its received sacrifices. Another instance: at a crossroads outside a Yoruba village a simple mound of earth is not a mortar pile, nor is it an accumulation of ant dredgings. One notes that a chicken is being sacrificed to it. Clearly this is extraordinary treatment to accord a mere bit of mud! Such speciality of treatment, distinguishing these things as exceptional among objects, comes about because the ends these things serve are not those simply of the body, as the ends of ordinary objects tend to be, but rather special ones. Indeed, the ends they serve are those of the state—in the case of the drum —and of the self. In ways that have always been most difficult to study, such things tend to gratify the human psyche. Thus the celt, investigation reveals, gains psychological power because it derives from the thunder god—it is the essence or seed or distillate of thunder; the drum is in some important sense the voice of the very soul of the Ashanti people; and the mud is a shrine to Eshu, the Yoruba god of indeterminacy. What better place to honor such a god than at a crossroads? One proceeds on a journey in greater confidence knowing that his choice of path has been presided over and validated by the blessings of the appropriate god.

Although in our culture we do not make sacrifices of blood to such special things, yet we too have analogous "objects." To them, Americans and Europeans and Japanese—for example—also offer "sacrifice." We may or may not write poems to them, but we lavish our resources upon their purchase and upkeep. And we house them in some of the grandest structures our culture produces, designed by our most gifted architects and executed in the most expensive of materials. But it is not only the housing of such works that is expensive. There are also the services they must have: insurance, guards to protect them against vandalism and theft, conservators to cure them of their ills and to maintain them in the greatest degree of health, specialists to mount them and place them in dramatically disposed and lighted displays.

The situation is somewhat the same in those cultures we think of as "primitive" or "tribal"—there is no satisfactory word by which to name them. Here whereas magnificence of housing may not so much be the case, *speciality* of housing characteristically tends to be; for such things are often, and perhaps even typically, kept in or near those honored and sacred places dedicated to the special needs of gods and spirits. Such pieces are attended, too—by priests or priestesses. And sacrifices are made in their behalf as well: their purchase requires the expenditure of scarce resources, and their upkeep is likely to demand the price of a libation of wine, or of the sacrifice of a chicken or goat. In addition, these pieces are often treated to cosmetics, bathed, and clothed. All this is honor due those "things" which intrude cosmic indifference or antipathy in order to serve man. Some of our own views concerning the functions of art are not significantly different, for we too think such things serve us: we think of the artwork as having therapeutic values. For example, we often see them as "expressing" our deep selves, thus divesting our psyches of perhaps dangerous emotions. Further, as the Ashanti royal drums might rally the Asantehene's people, so might the Black Madonna of Poland rally the Poles, and (on a somewhat more complex scale) the Louvre of France or the National Portrait Gallery of Britain tend to be focal points of intense national pride.

At one time, such things will stir us to patriotic action—"La Marseillaise," for instance. At other times they own the "power to chasten and subdue." We are outraged by their profanation; we stand in deference before them, speaking in hushed tones; and we honor them beyond measure. In tribal cultures, the behavior they evoke is not wholly different, save that the actions to which they drive people tend sometimes to be more exuberant than those of Americans: those who witness them might experience religious emotions, and on some occasions and in certain places might be driven even into states of possession and ecstasy.

Such things are not, at base, symbols of something else (a symbol being something that has arbitrary form and is held by convention to "stand for" something else); they *are* whatever they are. Human behavior before them tells us that. Indeed, using this simple, behavioral evidence as a criterion of classification helps us more markedly in our attempts to fit such phenomena into the schemes of human existence than centuries of attempts to "define *art.*" It is for this reason that I tend not to use the word "art"—save in a highly particular sense, as we shall subsequently see—speaking rather of such things as "works of affecting presence," denominating thereby the fact that they are special kinds of things ("works") which have significances not primarily conceptual (they are "affecting"), and which own certain characteristics that cause them to be treated more like persons than like things ("presence").

But all such works exist in a state of ambiguity, for if they own presence, if they are of the nature of person—which is what our behavior toward them argues—they are also of the nature of a thing. They are made through the same processes by which other things are made; the materials of which they are made are the same; and they are to be bought and sold.

They are in these respects, objects. But they are also subjects, being treated as human subjects are treated. And such works exist in a state of tension between these two poles: being subject and being object. It is perhaps in the energy of such interplay that a fundamental "power"—or energy—of the work of affecting presence is to be found.

In fact, "power" seems the most appropriate name for those distinctive though elusive properties which distinguish from all other sorts of things those in which we are here interested. It is the work's power which demands our attention; it is power which quickens us so that we greatly prize such things and, thus, so universally make them; and it is power which both requires and validates those sacrifices we exact of ourselves and of our goods in their behalf. Indeed, it is more useful—and certainly more appropriate to the study of a wide range of such kinds of things—to think of the nature of the aesthetic as being more rewardingly approached in terms relating to *power* than to *beauty,* for example.

At this moment in our study, we do not know what such power is, though we suspect its nature is more likely to be complex than simple, inasmuch as that often tends to be true of human phenomena. Thus the *power* of powered-things is likely to be of various aspects rather than of one only.

To search into the nature of a work's causal powers requires the wedding of two disciplines: anthropology and aesthetics. Anthropology is inevitable because if we are to pursue our understanding of a general human phenomenon, we must proceed to do so by perceiving common features beneath cultural diversities. Our study is rooted in aesthetics because our focus rests upon those properties of a work of affecting presence which distinguish it from all those other sorts of things which share "thingliness" with it but which are not works of such presence.

The best place to commence such an interdisciplinary study is to say that we use the word "art" with ambiguity. First, we name with it the "work of art," that elegant phenomenon in which we Europeans and Americans and Japanese—and so forth—take a kind of delight highly unusual among many others of the various families of man. This is to say that we value the work for how it looks or sounds or strikes the fancy rather than for what it does or what it *is.*

It is in a broader sense that one uses the term "art" when one says it is "universal." The interests of our understanding, therefore, require that we should disentangle these two meanings—one particular and the other "universal"—assigning distinctive and thus more useful terms to the two related but by no means identical phenomena. As is so often the case in our attempts to communicate one to the other, we find that identical terms for different phenomena inhibit thought by obscuring signal differences and thus subverting our attempts to understand.

A "work of art," in our Western sense, is an object or event caused to be "a work of art" by virtue of the fact that it abides in an estate of perceptible, moral, or psychological quality—of excellence. The *Mona Lisa,* for example, is caused to be a "great" and "powerful" work of art because of the excellence of its conception and execution, and not at all because it is a representation of a particular historical personage.

Yet there are cultures, for example, those in Black Africa, where the work is caused to be what it is—to own its power—precisely because of its "who-ness" or "what-ness," and not at all because of the excellence of its execution, morality, or expression. This is a point anthropologists and traditional aestheticians alike seem to miss, attempting instead to find "principles" of "beauty" or "harmony" or "virtue" or "rhythm" or "symmetry," whose exercise in excellence is presumed to be the cause of the thing's or event's becoming a "work of art," thus transferring to an alien culture the unexamined preferences of their own. An ancestor figure among the Dogon of Mali (plate 1) is what it is precisely because it enacts ancestors, and not because it may do so in a fashion we Westerners might deem of surpassing excellence or "beauty."

Works whose status as "work" is determined by virtue of what or who they are share with those works which are determined to be works because of their excellence the fact that they are both "things" which are not treated as other kinds of things (hoes and pots), but rather are accorded a kind of deference ordinarily reserved for persons. We shall subsequently examine what it is about such a work that causes it to be so treated; to have status (think only of the highly deferential treatment people accord such works, giving them sacrifice—whether this be of wealth, as in America and Europe, or of blood or food, as in Africa and Oceania); to have "personality"; and even to have "rights"—notably the right to continue undisturbed, for is not an act of violence against such a work held to be of a graver degree than the violent act perpetrated against an ordinary object?

It is clear that in order to proceed to study the work of affecting presence, we must abandon our previously unquestioned assumption that all works we call "art" are everywhere and at all times the same sort of phenomena, always endowed with identical and peculiarly "aesthetic" properties, and that these are invariably related to the creation of the good, the true, the beautiful, and the excellent. This view of the nature of the aesthetic holds that great art is, everywhere, responsive to identical human needs, and that those needs are—or ought to be—the same as those we in Europe and America conceive to be isolated and defined by our greatest works of art in the Western world. Art, this view maintains, has something to do with physical (rhythmic, symmetrical, technical, and so on), moral, and psychological excellences and with man's hankering after them. There is, thus (those of such persuasion maintain), a universal aesthetic—art is everywhere to be judged by common standards—and we can find these categories of excellence as "universals" in art the world over.

But in fact this is not true. We do not insist that the ways in which peoples organize their social systems either are or ought to be the same, nor that all economies do or should identically fix upon the same notion of how one ought to go about conserving scarce resources. Why, then, do we think that the achievement of *virtuosity* in the incarnation of some quality in a work is the universal *sine qua non* of art?

We must, rather, embrace an aesthetic pluralism. For I fear the fact of the matter is that observable aesthetic systems are as variable—from people to people of the same time, and from epoch to epoch—as social systems and economies. This is so not only with respect to the particular nature of what one conceives to be "beauty," let us say (and concerning those cultures where the achievement of beauty is the purpose of art), but even with respect to the question whether, in fact, "beauty" has anything at all to do with the case. As for "the good," what has it to do with a Mondrian? Further, such a work might be strikingly irrelevant to any notion of "truth" many of its viewers might hold; and further (to cite another characteristic frequently assigned to the aesthetic), it has no "meaning," in the sense that it might own a "storyline" that can be wholly or even adequately reformulated in words.

If one granted all this, one might still argue that it proves nothing more than that different standards of beauty prevail—from audience to audience within a culture, and from culture to culture. Even so, the defender of an aesthetic of beauty or excellence might go on to maintain that there are works in any culture which are more beautiful than others. One who thus argues might ask the following of me: "Of any given type of carving within a culture, why is it that a collector might choose one ancestor figure, rejecting another? Is it not because, within its own cultural terms—the terms of the 'beauty' of that culture—the piece he chooses is one he thinks to be more excellent than one he might reject?"

In some sense, this point would be well taken. Yet the fact remains that when a collector buys a piece of African sculpture for his collection, he is "transliterating" the presence of that work from the "orthography" of its native accents into that of his own. In the culture of the work's origin (let us presume it is from the Yoruba people), the piece a collector chooses might or might not have been greatly valued. But if it were the case that it had been greatly revered, then one must question whether that was due to the work's greater degree of perceptible virtuosity. One will find that the criterion for value in such a case lies rather in the efficacy with which the work exercised the cultural power assigned to its management. In short, it is not merely a matter of "different beauties"; it is rather that the arts of different cultures enact different kinds of notions concerning what it is desirable for the created work to achieve. From culture to culture, thus, there are different reasons why the work has power and owns presence, and differences therefore in the way the work is regarded. In general, *we* would never throw away a work of art, whereas the Dogon people of Mali often did.

In some of the world's cultures—our own, for example—an aesthetic of the quality of a work obtains. Now *quality* in a work is elusive. Indeed it is often the case that of two quite similar works, one will have that mysterious quality which will cause it to be a work of art, while the other will lack such a quality and thus miss inclusion in that honorific estate. One such quality whose achievement tends to cause the work to be honored with the designation "art," is *excellence,* as I have already said. Thus if a work is ill-done, it cannot in our culture (in general) be a work of art. Further, if it is derivative, it also cannot be art—or not very great art. Similarly, it cannot be art if it is fraudulent: a work painted by an imitator of Rembrandt, however excellent, is so far from art that it comes to be a kind of evil. (An official of the Metropolitan Museum of Art said of a work once thought to be ancient but then later judged to be modern that as a fraud it was like a vampire and ought to have a stake driven through its heart.)

Such prescriptions as these do not obtain among the Yoruba. Of two sets of twin figures, one of which may be beautifully carved in our judgment (and so to us a "work of art") and the other not ("not a work of art"), the Yoruba will not necessarily regard the former as more effective than the latter in the service of the ends for which both pairs of carvings exist and in terms of which their aesthetic qualities are to be determined. "Beauty," this is to say, does not *cause* the twin figure to be whatever it is that it is held to be. As for *uniqueness,* the traditional Yoruba would find this notion utterly alien to his understanding of such works. To him, styles and genres are socialized. The result of this is that the same style is repeated many times over in the execution of figures so alike one another—in looks, dimensions, identities, and functions—that perceptible distinctions among them are clearly of little importance, much as the variations in the pronunciation of a word do not destroy its meaning from one utterance to another. *Differences* among twin figures, for example, do not create the works; *similarities* do. Uniqueness thus also falls as a Yoruba aesthetic criterion. Further, could I carve such figures, I suspect the Yoruba would readily accept them. Thus goes authenticity!

In most general terms, and on purely observable, behavioral grounds, it is possible to distinguish two classes of works bearing presence: one class is of works bearing the presence either of identity (who or what the work is said to be) or of effective process (management of the universe); the other is of works bearing the presence of excellence. Works of the first class tend rather clearly to be of the nature of persons. They have both social role and status. Further, they manifest some of the same needs as a person—they must be fed, bathed, and often clothed. This is the aesthetic of invocation.

The works of the other class of presence are not dedicated to the management of the energies of the world, but only to the management of the energies of their own internal systems—their conflicts, harmonies, resolutions, and balances. These works are in their own ways as surely treated as entities as are the works of the first class. Yet they are not presences of persons (whether these be the incarnation of gods or of ancestors or of cosmic power), but rather presences of qualities and internal significances. This is the aesthetic of virtuosity.

Works of the aesthetic of invocation require the validation of investment by external power. Those of the aesthetic of virtuosity are autonomous internal systems whose qualities are neither augmented nor diminished by invocation. One may observe that, in general, works of invocation sometimes are not in-presence, whereas those of virtuosity always are (provided that they are not out of fashion). This is to say, for example, that a powerful secret-society mask in West Africa may very well have no reality of presence as it lies wrapped in cloth among the rafters of a house, but it becomes translated into glory when it is invoked in rite. A Monet, on the contrary, enjoys its condition of work-of-art at every instant of its being, so long as endures a culture within which its presence is acknowledged.

In contrast with the work of virtuosity, which is unitary—always whole and always "in power"—the work of the aesthetic of invocation is dualistic. This conclusion is to be reached upon one's realizing that the physical *thing*—the sculpture or the mask, for example—is one aspect, whereas the power that under appropriate conditions infuses it is another. When the object or event is in enactment, it is a "work"; when that same object or event is at rest, it is "not a work." The uninvoked object or event (the mask, the statue, the text, the music, the dance), that which in our aesthetic we call "the work," is in an aesthetic of invocation but an "item" in the work. Thus it is that when Western connoisseurs collect "African art," they collect not *works* but rather only *items*. When we think of the aesthetic of invocation, we from an aesthetic of virtuosity must not be beguiled by our own aesthetic but must hold in mind the distinction between *item* and *work*.

The work-in-invocation tends to exist in an ambient of time; what has happened to it in the past is portion of its being. It never exists in space alone as a work-in-virtuosity may. This is due to the fact that the invoked work exists only in performance. Some works in the aesthetic of invocation exist forever invoked—always, in effect, in performance. A fetish, for example, lives in the residual power of past sacrifices and exists ever in the condition of bearing witness to contracts made before it (see the oath-taking image, plate 2, and Thompson 1978). The power in a sculpture of invocation is, thus, not only absent or present, but when present is likely to be *variably* so.

There are other differences between the two kinds of works. The invoked work tends to be dedicated to the validation of man, whereas the work of virtuosity tends to be dedicated to the validation of itself. The invoked work tends to be communal, whereas the virtuosic work tends to be individual. The former therefore moves in the direction of the powers of the gods or of society and may thus be called "metaphysical," whereas the latter is to be thought of as "psychological," spinning its energies not between gods and man but wholly between itself and its witness. The task of the virtuosic work is not to move immortals but to move man. The chief means of achieving this end are to be found in the execution of a work in a state of mastery, whether this be of content, techniques, feelings, or of all these taken together.

But we must not imagine that in works of invocation, virtuosity may not in some sense be present; at the very least such works enjoy virtuosity with respect to the generation or invocation and management of energy. Nor must we think that energy is necessarily alien to works created within an aesthetic of virtuosity; we speak of the "verve" of a work, for example, or more forthrightly of its "power" or "energy." But the former kind of work is not to be defined by its virtuosity, nor the latter by its energy.

Works under an aesthetic of invocation (let us think of an important mask) are conceived to be physical loci of extramortal energies which may be so strong that they can and often do vitiate or destroy the piece which hosts them. Further, the fact of the matter is that such power is not fixed, but is variable in its degree. When it wanes it must be augmented. And when through long indwelling it destroys its piece, as inevitably will happen if the item is wooden, then the piece must be replaced.

That which is the aesthetic cause—the principle of affecting presence —may or may not be present within the work of invocation at any given time; if present, it may be so either weakly or strongly. That a given work should be of one sort at one time (a work of affecting presence when invoked) and of a different sort at another time (when it is not invoked) is thus a further characteristic of the aesthetic of invocation.

The aesthetic of virtuosity originates in the freeing of the work of affecting presence from dependence upon the energies of gods and other external sources, committing it instead to a dependence upon the more reliable though less mighty abilities of man. Its focus lies not in embodying who-ness or what-ness, but how-ness; not in managing power, but in perpetrating excellence; not in establishing the general, but in exalting the particular. Because man's understanding of the universe is less given to change than his fashions of excellence, the aesthetic of invocation has been less hospitable to fluctuations and fashions than has the aesthetic of virtuosity—as we may conclude from an examination of the relative stability of so-called primitive art over the last two centuries, in contrast with the profusion of styles and movements that have evolved over the same period in Western art.

The history of the aesthetic of virtuosity has exploited a spectrum of excellences of concentration: from an emphasis upon virtuosity of "form" at the expense of "content" (the rococo), to an emphasis upon a like mastery of content over form (primitivism); from the presentation of the known (Michaelangelo's *Pieta*), to the presentation of the unknown—and, indeed, the unknowable (as we may discern in many of the aesthetic new-nesses being experimented with in our own day, e.g., minimalism). Indeed, one may interpret successive stages in Western art history as the discovery and efflorescence of new virtuosities, or of new associations or interpretations of known ones.

Differing virtuosities define differing artistic movements. Sometimes more than one virtuosity emerges. Thus, it is as futile to expect to find *one* aesthetic of virtuosity in a population as complex as that of twentieth-century America as it is to expect that all the arts of all the peoples of the world are similarly concerned with, let us say, beauty.

The aesthetic dualism of the item in the work of invocation requires that it sometimes *is* and at other times *is not* in-presence. This "on" and "off" ontology is a function of its being sacrificed to or not; of its being attended with food, clothing, and cosmetics, or alternatively unattended; of its being embellished or not embellished, and so on. The enactment of such patterned variations falls within what I have called "syndesis": the basic process of apprehending and constructing the world. Together with synthesis, synde-sis constitutes the totality of those modes in which the human conscious-ness apprehends and enacts the world and the self—through a process of oppositions and eventuations (synthesis) on the one hand, and through a process of accretion (syndesis) on the other.

The synthetic work owns inherent principles of *development.* It pro-ceeds through the execution and resolution of opposites. Its successive units are different from one another; and insofar as successive phases grow out of prior ones, the synthetic work is linear. The syndetic work, on the other hand, grows in accordance with extrinsic principles; its *growth* is through repetition of the same or of a small inventory of similar units. It does not *develop;* there is no entailment of the subsequent to be found in the prior. If a drummer beats a pattern of two beats against three, he repeats that pattern over and over again, and the happening of no particular subsequent beat can be said to have been entailed by its predecessor. The duration of the music, and ultimately the definition of the work's wholeness, is attributable to extrinsic causes. Only circumstance, and often whim, determine (in modern, European art, for instance) the location or the nature of an element in many collages. Finally, the synthetic tends to be secular—though it is not neces-sarily so; and the syndetic tends, though not necessarily, to be sacred or affiliated with the sacred.

It is interesting to note, in passing, other syndetic attributes of the work of virtuosity: the prestige that accrues to the owner of a virtuosic work syndetically enriches him; further, syndesis insists its value in the art museums and music auditoriums, where such works are most often encountered, for in such places the work is brought into additive relationship with other works, either by the same or by different artists. There is, in the behavioral context, something even of the syndesis of invocation to the museum: the opening nights when the guests are libated in honor of the works, and ritual foods are consumed; the days thereafter when the critics who were in attendance either admit or deny the work's installation into the mysterious world of "art." Invocation and virtuosity are not to be divorced one from another. The invoked work owns, at the very least, virtuosity of the ability to cause, and the work of virtuosity owns the power to move one's sensibilities. Both invocation and virtuosity are means to power. They are, in their respective cultures, among the necessary conditions for power, that power which yields presence.

Some scholars study the work of affecting presence in its historical settings, searching out the identities of personages, places, and things depicted, or the "hand" who executed the paintings—relating these painters one to another in careful genealogies—and studying such other aspects of the works' time-dimensions as may engage them. Others equally seriously direct their efforts toward ascertaining economic, social, or political variables, or try to discern in a body of works the "spirit of the times." Still other researchers are interested chiefly in the excellences of works.

But such scholars—however much they might increase our historical and social knowledge—do not teach us why or how the work of affecting presence *is* both a presence *and* affecting. Thus, there is another kind of scholar, one who strives to study the work precisely in terms of its distinctive properties, its essential differences from all other kinds of human artifacts, events, and affairs. Such workers strive to see the work as an estate of human consciousness, a unique binding together in human cognition both of objective phenomena and of subjective values concerning them. I myself am this latter sort of worker, believing that in certain kinds of processes—invocation and virtuosity, syndesis and synthesis, for instance—are to be found those energies which give the work both affect and presence.

The word "powers" is responsive to this persuasion, naming the fact that the work owns some kind of ability—of efficacy of affect. In both invocation and virtuosity power is summoned. In both, the energies of syndesis increase power through donation, enriching the item (in invocation) through prayer, sacrifice, and tribute until presence is brought about. In the works of the aesthetic of virtuosity, syndetic enrichment is to be seen in the donations of the work's singularity and of the enormity of its creator's genius. In each of these cases, if I were to speak of the work's powers, I would mean its ability to stand in an estate of increased affect owing to its having been (or *being*) added to. And insofar as that which is added is of the nature of essences as defined by the culture—the essence (blood) of a victim or of a prayer, in one case; the essence which is the distillation of unique genius, in the other—both are packed with the most powerful distillates of the consciousness itself. These essences may thus be seen as *investments* in the work: the proper item is invoked in the appropriate rite, which defines the necessary and sufficient conditions for the invocation of a god; the particular genius of Picasso in execution of the painting and the singularity of a primarily blue palette in the unusual mood of the piece all enrich the guitar player into a work of art. The donational (syndetic) nature of the act of genius is perhaps best seen in the notion that a lesser painter could have painted a blue guitarist but failed to achieve an analogous intensity of work. Genius does not make the work more "guitar player," but it does make it more "art."

Yet these investments are not to be seen as only of a well-known and readily recognizable contents of the world. The simple fact of the existence of a nonrepresentative work (let us consider one of abstract expressionism) argues that there are powers other than such "substantive" ones, powers which lie beyond the mere depiction of the world's recognizable "nouns" and "verbs." In an "action painting," it is less work than *constituting of work* which is of affect and presence. In brief, some of the powers of a work— and those that will concern us in this study—are those which establish it in its specific (i.e., of the nature of *species*) efficacies, in those estates which are common to all works—which is to say those powers which cause the work, wherever it might be found, to exist in affecting presence.

The powers of the work constitute the fulcrum upon which presence teeters, sometimes dipping toward absolute object-ness (a giant ice bag, for instance), at other times tipping toward transcendence (e.g., Lipschitz's *Prometheus*). Power may vary in its indwelling of a work, being weak or strong in its density, magnitude, and elegance.

The *presence* achieved in a work is the sum total of all those powers that excite it, quickening it from its core to its flanks, charging it with significant perusals—the affirmations and interrogations—of consciousness. Thus, inasmuch as power is variable in degree and in intensity, it follows that so also is presence. If the presence of the work is such that the work is treated after the fashion of a human person, then it also follows that such powers as the work owns must be very like those owned by human persons. The problem of defining the powers of the work thus becomes one of finding those respects in which processes of work and person are the same. Insofar as it is clear that these identities are neither physiological nor anatomical, then—given but the three simple choices—they are to be seen as psychological.

The work of affecting presence—sharing psychological processes with persons—sometimes seems as much to apprehend its witness as its witness apprehends it. This phenomenon is especially apparent in the instance of a danced mask. I myself have felt scrutinized to my essence, turned nearly into an object before the insistent confrontations of a mask danced. It is much the same with a portrait—this is easy enough to see. But the case becomes more difficult when we consider a landscape. And, indeed, does it not appear to be of a completely different order when we leave depiction to enter into the world of abstract expressionism, or depart the visual entirely, journeying instead into the intergalactic spaces of Cage's sound or of Pound's recondite lexical images? Still we know that something is abroad there, something akin to but yet not ourselves—something existent there, *something being.*

The work of affecting presence is a phenomenon of consciousness, and any theory of the nature of the aesthetic must at base be inextricable from a theory of the nature of the consciousness itself. The condition of the consciousness in which the work of affecting presence abides is one of action. The work thus owns a property much like that of man himself, who also abides in action while he holds the world in his apperception of it. The power of work and the power of man are thus at base similarly active estates of the consciousness; this defines a property man and work share. And further, is it not the case concerning both man and work existing in such sentience that much, and sometimes all, of the lived moment defies language's abilities to replicate or report? The feeling that we seem somehow witnessed by the work of affecting presence is testimony to the nature of this power that both man and work own.

Whatever else it is, human consciousness is both more complex and more subtle—more inscrutable before our explicit awareness—than we seem ordinarily to suppose. Further, what we already know of it from the works of students of the human psyche is not likely to help us very much in our search. For these thinkers and scholars have identified and worked with such aspects of the consciousness as have seemed pertinent to the achievement of their particular ends: coming to understand the learning processes or treating the "mind" in need of therapy, lest the anxious savageries of existence overwhelm and submerge the person.

Certainly I wish to make no pretense of appearing to offer here a general view of the full consciousness. On the contrary, just like psychologists and psychiatrists, I am concerned only with such aspects of that vital and complex synergy that will help us understand the nature of the work of affecting presence.

To be sure, man is unique among his fellow animals in numerous respects. The one which for the moment interests us is the fact that he has learned how to make behavior an end in itself rather than a means to achieving food, safety, and propagation. Critical to this achievement was his attainment of insight into the processes of the world such that he reached an understanding concerning the distinction between cause and effect. No longer was the world simply *results,* concerning which he might do little. Instead, he saw that a relationship of functional dependence exists between the two, and he learned that by varying one, he might alter the other. Further, he developed ways of conveying meaning with both reliability and complexity, so that the odyssey of his cause-effect experiences might be shared and learning might occur. The result of these innovations was a behavioral revolution, such that man became the first animal to invent significantly alternative behaviors to respond to common imperatives. Still, he was not delivered over into the behavioral chaos of utter diversity and unpredictability.

In man's expanding repertoire of behavioral options, two forces of his consciousness are simultaneously at work. One of these has demanded that he enact behaviors common to his kind, while the other has required that he become individual, so that he might mark the world with the historical fact of his having been present in it. Thus all societies of men have families, though some be matrilineal and others patrilineal; and all men have languages, even though these might be unintelligible from group to group. Further, on either side of such institutionalized behavior, there are additional behaviors, some more basic—more common to our kind (that is to say "specific")—and some others more individual. For instance, from culture to culture man owns certain kinds of communications which tend to be cross-culturally understandable. One thinks of a smile, an embrace, a question formulated in the eye, or a glint of assent. These are supracultural behaviors. In the second place one thinks of those subtle glances lovers pass, intimating shared privacies; one thinks of the hermetically isolated individualization of the psychotic; one thinks of the unique genius of the innovative artist or physicist.

Further, the consciousness of Homo sapiens is characterized by a complexity of past configurations, some of which—at the *top,* as it were—are identifiable to him as personal (these are "memories"), whereas others lie so *deeply* that they defy articulation into the discrete syllables of positive knowledge. These latter ones are of his kind. One thinks of the events of yesterday, in the first instance, and in the second, of those obscure disturbances of the soul that sometimes trouble our sleep. One thinks of such deep mammalian behaviors as suckling the young, and of deeper ones yet: enacting relationships. But one also thinks of the memorialization in art of the most fleeting tenderness. More than any others of the biological kingdoms, mankind stands transfixed between the mighty gravities of the universal from which he derives, and of the particular toward which he is driven.

The human consciousness, then, teeters between the general and the specific, the deeps and the surfaces. Consciousness may exist at every conceivable point in these subtle continua. Some of these points we are specifically aware of; others we perhaps shall never summon forth into known particularity. But the latter no less than the former are constitutive of human consciousness.

Man's consciousness is simultaneously capable of both change and stability. And though we sleep with an awareness to the same inchoate terrors that trouble the fitful sleeping of the wolf, so do we rise to the heady formulations of poetry. An order of consciousness once having been established becomes available to all mankind. Each of us simultaneously repeats in his individual being both the evolution of the consciousness of his generic lineage as well as the excitement of most recent novelty.

As it is with man himself, so is it with the powers that invest the work of affecting presence. The fact that the consciousness is a confluence of general and specific powers is a fact of life; the fact that such powers may be incarnated within a work is a fact of man. Both man's and work's particularities are simultaneously and variously cultural and individual.

I shall try to isolate and identify some of the more obvious orders of these common fountainheads of power of man and work, commencing with the most obscure and working toward the most obvious, proceeding from the most general to the most particular. All that is general, a power of man's lineage—either of his *kind* or of his *culture*—I shall call "diaconsciousness" (a portmanteau word made from "diachronic consciousness"); and all that is particular—the surface of his knowing of the world in its individuality —I shall call the "synconsciousness" (from "synchronic consciousness").

The first power that invests the work of affecting presence is the power of analogicity. This power is to be found in the mere fact of bringing into being. That which one causes to come into being may be the disposition of his body or physiognomy, as in attitudes of threat or looks of resignation; or it may be an object or an event in the world outside, quite independent of the facilities of the human body.

The next power of affecting presence is the power of subjectivity, and beyond that is the power of those estates we call "the mythic": on the one hand, immemorial inventions of person, place, thing, event, and process which, investing the work of affecting presence, lend it that generality of engagement with the human subject which we sometimes call "the universal" in the phenomena of the aesthetic; and on the other hand, the power of the simple generative energies which beget a given culture in its particular distinctiveness. The final power of the work of affecting presence is the one of particularity, of being of that class or of that individuality—whichever, depending upon whether the aesthetic with which we are concerned be that of a culture in which the socialization of forms is valued and executed, or that of a culture in which the individuality of artist and of work come to own the greatest value. All these, orchestrated into a synergistic unity, comprise part of that deep font of sentience whose powers dwell within a work as clearly as they do within each human person, and in which—as one standing before a mirror—waits the reflected eye of the human consciousness, gazing out upon itself from the work of affecting presence.

Each of these orders of power is a denomination of human sentience. Each is the presence of a power of realizing the world—thing from nonthing, subject from nonsubject, myth from nonmyth, and that which is cultural from that which is alien. The work of affecting presence exists, therefore, as a point of vital intersection in the complex nexus of the powers—the processes of *being enacted*—of all these orders of knowing and being. Such is the estate of the consciousness that the work of affecting presence holds in action.

That the work of affecting presence appears sometimes to *apperceive us* stems from the fact that it embodies those same powers of causing awareness of self and world which stir and validate the consciousness of man himself. We touch here upon the marvel of man's incredible abilities to project his own being into the world, so that he might make it as nearly wholly hospitable as possible to the needs which grow out of his determination to live and to thrive therein. Such monuments of his consciousness form not only his works of affecting presence, but his gods as well. As the aesthetic of invocation argues, any division between works and divinities is tenuous. (Thus perhaps have gods sometimes forbidden them.)

The powers of the aesthetic we have thus far observed are those of: (1) binding together an object and a value in affect such that (2) investment occurs, and this through the processes either of (3) donation, which is to say *syndesis,* or (4) opposition and resolution, i.e., *synthesis;* furthermore, as a subset of the powers of syndesis, (5) virtuosity may be definitive of the work. Virtuosity, we must note, is not restricted to the aesthetic generated of the dynamics of synthesis, but may be found bringing power into being in syndetic works as well (see plate 3, where a bowl excitingly enacts a virtuosity of syndetism and is alien to investment with the powers of invocation). These powers are all effectuating of presence, which is the sum total of all powers, whether inherent (the mask invoked into power of presence through rite) or ascribed (the mask in an American museum, transposed into an alien aesthetic system). Their effectuations are active properties, as active in works of an aesthetic of virtuosity—where they conspire to hold an estate of the consciousness in perpetual apprehension—as in works of an aesthetic of invocation—where the processes of effectuation do not abide in the work but are evanescent, to be performed and subsequently repeated over and over again.

The nerves of the work of affecting presence reach into those same obscure recesses of human being as those of religion. The arteries of presence and their throb and pressure are synaptical with belief. The process of the affecting presence is the process of bringing work into the powers of being, of making the hidden visible, the latent manifest, the inaudible audible, the stilled dynamic—of making the intransigent tractable. It is greatly suggestive of the act of Adam, commanded to name the animals of the world in order that for him they might *come to be.* The belief that nourishes presence nourishes and celebrates our being in the world.

2

THE POWERS OF THE ANALOGIC

Both syndesis and synthesis are basic processes in the commission of acts and the creation of objects which altogether constitute the human consciousness' enactment of self and world.[1] These are not the only processes of that order of basis. The disciplines of the work in its perhaps more simply sensuous dimensions are as well, whether the work (let us use sculpture as an example) reach maximally into space, seeking to explore the outmost periphery of the possibilities of its physical existence, as in a multiarmed, dancing Siva; or whether, contrariwise, it hunker after a deep center of gravity, hidden within its viscera, as tends to be the case among African figures (see the Waja figure, plate 4). The former of these conditions one calls "extension," and the latter "intension." Similarly basal are "continuity" and "discontinuity," the conditions in which either the discreteness of the structures of contiguous parts is emphasized—as in Javanese dance, emphasis is placed upon the articulation of the forms of sequential positions in space rather than upon the grammar of their transitions (discontinuity)—or else the follow-through of these serial components is stressed, toward the end of creating a taut continuum (continuity). These disciplines together with the dynamics of either syndesis or synthesis order all those works of affecting behavior with which we are concerned, whether these occur outside in the world or in the innermost reaches of *felt* time and space. I should note that "discipline" as I have used it above is meant to

1. I am informed in this chapter by Henry Glassie's magisterial essay, "Meaningful Things and Appropriate Myths: The Artifact's Place in American Studies" (1977). Most notably I am indebted to him for discussions concerning the relationship between shape and meaning, and what "meaning" might be said to be in the work of affecting presence.

designate an active estate: the work of affecting presence is to be understood as *being* intensive, *being* continuous, and so on.

Owing to the fact that these processes are so elementary, they abide in an estate of unchallengeable rightness, owning a sense of being "natural." They thus exist in cultures in an ambient of value. And one may speak of their *vitality,* therefore, in that value gives life to the consciousness as blood does to the body. Further, as meaning is the "value" of a word—or as a particular number is the "value" of a symbol (let us say as, in a given case, "three is the value of X")—so is affect the value of the rightness of the world. Thus all these processes I have mentioned are *in affect*—they are *sources* of affect. The *powers* of a work are its enactments of affect. *The* power of a work is the sum total of its various powers and is to be seen (when so used) as the equivalent of *presence* itself. Syndesis, intention, and continuity, one suspects, are more ancient to human consciousness than their alternatives.

We encounter these disciplines enacted in the first affecting works mankind seems to have created, in the Upper Paleolithic caves of France and Spain. They also dominate the works of many among the world's "tribal" peoples—in each of the world's major identifiable culture areas. The depth from which syndesis arises is suggested by the fact that it is the common logic of our deepest dreams. And concerning the originality of intension and continuity, one need cite only their pervasion, along with syndesis, of the works of affecting presence of nearly all "tribal" peoples.

There is thus a sense of primacy to syndesis, intension, and continuity. In syndesis, this primacy stems from the fact that the process is both the inventorying of things and events of the world, and the logic of juxtaposing them which governs their simplest, copulative predications one upon another. The power of the syndetic is perhaps thus the power of man's first projections of his psychic focus into the world beyond his body, removing it from a self that is but a succession of present moments into a self that exists in a time no longer simply that of periodicities given by physiology and in a space whose only significant contents are no more than food, sex, and enmity. The power of the mighty evolution that brought him into being, that shift from bondage to a sole reality of body-in-world to the greater freedom of self-in-world-and-time, this is a portion of the basal power of the syndetic.

The primacy of intension and continuity rests in their direct presentation of the strength of upright things (the tree, the body, the phallus); the intensive seems to enact straightforward strength; and continuity, the virtue of successivity in generations, selves, crops. Together they create a profound dynamic of the *being* of the work of affecting presence, which is resonant with primary powers—with the powers of being processes and of being primaries.

Synthesis, syndesis, continuity, discontinuity, intension, extension—these are the elementary processes of all human acts, whether those of the body simply; those of the body extended or amplified through weapons and tools; or those of the psyche, works of conceptual and of affecting presence.

But we may not lose sight of the fact that these dynamics are *of* things and events, and things and events as such are even more ancient in the consciousness whose base man shares with other of the more complex animals. These dynamics, in short, are hominid syndeses upon the *things* known to the lower mammals. We may thus suspect that the deepest roots of the power in which we are interested descend into the nature of *the thing* itself. It is only after we have examined this suspicion that we shall be able to address the question of the thing-in-presence. Certainly it is to presence rather than to thing in itself that our inquiry is directed.

With their bodies all animals perform repertoires of acts which define and effectuate in space, time, and process their presence in the world. They hunt or graze or trap, they propagate, they defend themselves, and they go about the business of bringing their young to physical independence. All these are bare, brutish actions. But the higher animal forms do more as well. They similarly enact with their bodies certain postures which convey information enforcing that kind of behavior proper to their kind. They might bare teeth one at another, warning that some act of another is unacceptable; or making loving sounds, they might approach one another. Indeed, behavior of this category may become quite complex. Consider the case of the wolf, as reviewed by Gregory Bateson.[2] Both the male and female adults of the wolf pack participate in the weaning of the young. This they do by pressing down with open jaws upon the neck of a hungry youngster who seeks to nurse. When later one of the junior males, grown to sexual matu-

---

2. Gregory Bateson, "Problems in Cetacean and Other Mammalian Communication," in *Steps to an Ecology of Mind* (1972). I am indebted to the author for the wolf example; for the concept of the analogic and the digital; the relational content of the analogic (though I have extrapolated from mammalian analogical behavior in general to that of man in particular—especially the notion of tools and art as analogic and relational); and my understanding of the nature of dolphin communication.

rity, might violate a female with respect to whom the senior adult male of the pack owns sexual rights, the latter offended creature will discipline the junior male by pressing down upon his neck with open jaws. The senior male, Bateson concludes, is thus enacting his superiority over the younger male.

Animals thus conduct two different kinds of bodily behaviors: those relating to their well-being as individual physical creatures, and those pertaining to the conduct of their social life. We can say that social action requires the passing of information, whereas comfort-behavior seems less likely to do so. One must also note that these two kinds of behavior exist on a continuum, so that one behavior shades into the other. Thus is it sometimes difficult to classify a given action as one or the other.

Both of these behaviors are "analogic," which is to say that both have the very shapes of the information they convey. In the case of the wolf the information is dominance. The senior wolf's prerogative of unchallenged aggressive behavior toward his junior is the very stuff of domination. His behavior is not a *name* of dominion, it *is* dominion. It exists in real action, having real enactments of real magnitudes.

Such actions as these, whether for creature well-being or for socialization, are agencies of the creature's execution of his existence. And all the behaviors they enact are both basic to and given as definitive of the individual's kind and are critical to the kind's continuity. Further, they are behaviors of value and affect: in procreation the creature reduces a compelling drive; in feeding he experiences the satisfaction of defeating hunger; in disciplining his juniors he asserts his notions concerning the rightness of conduct. All these behaviors exist in a field of obligatory rightness. There is an inevitability to their doing. And it is good—let us say—for a wolf to enact wolfness. The body thus enacts the prime values of the kind.

Man similarly enacts analogic estates with his body: he communicates acceptance and rejection, desire and revulsion through "body language." But man has done more. He has externalized his analogic behavior, creating it free in both time and space. The plasticities of space (the *here* and *there,* the materials and shapes of objects in space) and time (*then* and *now* and *to come*) enormously enlarged the possibilities of his behavior. Human history has been the history of human exploitation of the potentialities of spatial and temporal analogics.

The power of the corporeal analogic is the power of the enactment of the body in the grip of its imperatives, and the power of the externalized analogic is the power of enacting self in world and time. The analogic is a primal necessity to being. In man's case, it is one of his mammalian *givens,* and as such it owns the power of deep affect. It requires some recognition of this affective power of the analogic to explain the power of material possessions, in some among our kind reaching the intensities and inappropriateness of neuroses.

So we might readily suppose that the rock which augmented the lethal efficacy of ancient man's hand shared the affect accompanying the attack in which it was used. And that chipped surface of stone flake which let man cut skins must have participated in the suffusing satisfaction of warm clothing. And can we not also imagine that the arrow loosed in flight might have taken to itself a little of the anticipations which flew with it toward the prey it was directed to kill? And do we not, in point of fact, see something of this affect that things might bear when we recall that during the Middle Ages swords were inscribed with legends proclaiming their might? And when we call to mind that even today we personify and name ships and guns, and imbue the thingly world with obdurate and often perverse powers of personalized efficacy (as we personify, then curse, the rock that stubs our toes)?

But the analogic projects not the self alone. It establishes the self *in relationships:* as the wolf's behavior, Bateson says, asserts his relationships to his junior, so in a similar way does a tool assert man's relationship to a task, and an ancestor figure or a church proclaim his relationship to the powers of the divine. These relationships are transactions in efficacy—in supremacy, inferiority, or equity—no matter whether, in man's case, they exist among individuals of his sort, or between him and the objects, the events, and the processes of the world. The relating power of the analogic constitutes some of its further power.

We should note in passing that man has identified a further universe of relationships which he enacts not analogically but symbolically—or, in Bateson's term, "digitally." Digital behavior involves the use of actions which communicate *not* through analogic means, but rather through actions which have arbitrary shapes that do not constitute meaning but serve instead to advise us that (accepting the terms of the convention) meaning is present. In the analogic there is no disparity between shape and meaning; in the digital, or symbolic, there always is. "Big" and "little" are such digital terms, for instance, and there is no relationship between their forms and the meanings they convey. Indeed, "big" as a lexical item (or at least as an orthographic one) is smaller than "little" is.

The digital names but does not enact powers. Indeed, we have expressions of this when we speak of "raising a number to the *power* of another sign." But it is the power of the analogic that is of interest to us here, for the aesthetic is a special condition of the analogic, sharing in its generic powers of affect and relationship, as well as in certain subsequent powers of facticity—powers of the thing; powers of the self extended into the world; and powers of the subjectivity of the work of affecting presence. These are the unique powers of the aesthetic.

The things of the universe of the projected analogic, like those of the corporeal analogic, relate the self to the obdurate, factual world of the presence of other selves, other creatures, other needs, and thingly multiplicities. The universe of the analogic is the primary one of man's being, the one to which in largest measure the digital makes reference (or in poetry asserts). As the stage of man's behavior is so greatly enlarged in consequence of his externalization of analogic behavior, so also are the domains of the kinds of his behavior. Thus in addition to analogic behaviors of perpetuation and communication (such as wolves have), man adds diversion, prestige, and celebration. In the last chapter of this volume we shall see that it is to celebration that the analogics of affecting presence belong. (This is not to suggest that works of affecting presence therefore are without functions in any other of the domains of consciousness. Quite the contrary: such works may communicate, perpetuate—as fertility or antiwitchcraft charms—and delight.) To understand celebrative relationships as the definitive process of the analogics of affecting presence, we must examine the whole realm of the externalized analogic.

The powers of the externalized analogic lie in its having been made, and in its being something in its own terms, with its own purposes and its own efficacies. They lie also in fulfilling and extending man—bonding him and the outside world. The respect man gives the made-thing is enormous. We are known by our things; they accord us prestige. And we take the greatest care of them. We build museums for all sorts of things: paper, automobiles, tools, art. It is only the inscrutable power of the thing that explains the extraordinary phenomenon of our throwaway culture. For the greatest enactment of one's personal power is to swell his sense of self by sucking into it the power of things consumed. It is an ancient syndetism.

There are further testimonies in behavior to the thing's power. There is the evidence of the thing suddenly invested with intent when the hammer bruises the thumb. In other days, a Javanese man might never draw his kris unless he provide it with blood to drink. We see the power of the thing when we use it for sacrifice, as in the once prodigious potlatches of the Indians dwelling along the Northwest Coast of North America.

Sometimes the power of the thing becomes somehow distorted or detached, and then magic results. Magic is a property of the thing-as-thing and not of the things as affecting presence; of the *thing-objective,* not of the *thing-subjective.* Magic is a power of the thing-as-thing. Generalized, the ring becomes not an ornament but a changer of one's fate—though yet a ring. The power of the thing in magic is ascribed and not inherent. It is the genie that is its presence—a prisoner who would escape, and not an ineluctable subjectivity.

Whether the work be of the aesthetic of invocation or of the aesthetic of virtuosity, and even though it be informed with presence—such that it enjoy some of the prerogatives and prestige of a person—yet it is also a thing, and it is as inextricable from its thingliness as it is from its presence. The thingliness of things-in-presence is that property they share with things-as-such. Thus, a consideration of thingliness is critical if we are to understand the differences between thing and work, if we are to discern those special powers that together override mere thingliness and eventuate into the work of affecting presence, distinguishing such powers from the powers of simple, thingly analogicity.

Now we usually think a book is a thing; so, too, some object whose identity is obscure to us, as well as a rock, a hammer, a Rodin sculpture. We do not seem, in ordinary discourse, to hold a dance to be a thing, or a conversation, or a poem, or a musical work. *Things,* in our common parlance, tend to occur in space, whereas we tend *not* to think of as things those happenings of time—events. Further, events audible are (according to folk taxonomy) seldom *things* (they are *sounds* or *noises*), whereas things palpable always are (if they be not a person or a known animal). Smells are never things, either, yet what we can see either may or may not be a thing. Now, in that the phenomena in which we are interested—works of affecting presence—are both "things" and "events" and are sufficiently diverse (as to their visibility, palpability, audibility, etc.) as to confound us in hairsplitting over whether, for example, the palpability of the dancer might not make the dance a thing rather than an event, I shall denote as "things" all phenomena which are not biologically living and which enjoy perceptible existence in the outside world.

It is further true that there are things that occur as given in nature, such as rocks and thunderstorms and gentle evenings; and then there are those made by man. I use the word "made" with some degree of latitude, so that I might include also those things given by nature that man adopts as such to his needs—for example, a flat rock taken to pound a stake, or one thought to contain mighty potencies. It is the category of things made by man and which are shape-constituted—of which a hammer is an instance, as also are a portrait, an act of crossing oneself, and all acts of "body language"—in which we are interested.

Things that are analogic (shape-constituted) are of more ancient ancestry in animal behavior (e.g., aggressive acts) than are things that are digital. Further, things that are analogic are *nonarbitrary* in shape or process, but they are necessary, which is to say that they are as they must be if they are to be what they are supposed to be. This may be the case either in point of objective fact (a screwdriver) or by cultural fact (as at Mass when the elevation of the Host and the invocation of the Holy Spirit create the Host into Presence). If either configuration or process is varied, the analogic thing cannot be that which it otherwise is. But those that are digital have shapes that are not *necessary;* they are as they are by convention and are thus *arbitrary.*

Things that are digital are relatively freely substitutable—one can say "house," "domicile," or "hut." They can substitute either for an analogic estate (that is, they can refer to it), or they can describe it, or report how it is achieved or for another digital estate (e.g., "Einstein's theory"); they are also amenable to translations into other codes—the oral may be written, the written may be spoken. Though the digital may account the analogic with great complexity and subtlety (it may not in any significant sense *substitute* for it), the analogic may never account for the digital, nor may it ever comment upon itself—as the digital may. The analogic and the digital may be syndetically joined (as X-crossed boards by tracks "mean" a railroad crossing, or as a blue veil on a female statue, in a church, "means" Blessed Virgin). Such joinings are called "icons."

Under certain circumstances, the analogic thing may be substituted with another analogic thing. We may have either functional or formal substitutes. Pounding, for example, may be achieved by using either a flat rock or a hammer—a case of functional substitutions. In formal substitutions (once more considering *pounding*), one may use either a ball-peen hammer or a claw hammer.

When the analogic thing is also a work of affecting presence, either substitutability or nonsubstitutability may obtain. Substitutability is to be encountered chiefly in an aesthetic of invocation, where forms tend to be socialized. Thus one mask of a given sort (let us say Yoruba Gelede masks, plates 5–8) may substitute for another of the same sort. (However a mask of sort "A" [a Gelede] may not substitute for a mask of another sort [e.g., an Egungun].) In the instance of nonsubstitutability, chiefly to be encountered among works in the aesthetic of virtuosity, however, the case is wholly different. A Picasso painting of a woman standing before a mirror is not the same as a Renaissance Flemish work on the same theme.

But it is not simply the case that things are either substitutable or nonsubstitutable. There are substitutable things variously tinged with nonsubstitutability, and nonsubstitutable things for which some order of substitutability exists. As an instance of the first, think of a hammer to which great value is attached—one used by a great craftsman, for instance. Its owner may very well feel he cannot drive a nail as satisfactorily with any other instrument. Or consider the silver hammer used to break a papal seal upon a pope's death. It is not that no other hammer could be used to achieve the simple physical results; it is rather that there is a propriety which makes this silver hammer's use nonsubstitutable. One might find an example of the nonsubstitutable tinged with substitutability in the instance of a decorator who may simply want "flowers" in a particular spot; it might make no difference whether they be painted by Van Gogh or Monet.

Both nonsubstitutable and substitutable things may be used as means toward the achievement of specific ends. A rock or hammer may be used to break something; a mask may be used to invoke the presence of a spirit. But it is things of the order of the nonsubstitutable that tend to be ends in themselves. Which is, of course, not to say that all nonsubstitutable things are such ends (e.g., the silver hammer of the Vatican—which is nonsubstitutable except by another silver hammer, should the present one be lost—is not an end in itself; and the class "Gelede masks" is not an end in itself, although each of its invocations into presence *is* an end). This is to say that among all things, only those that—being nonsubstitutable—are ends-in-themselves and works of affecting presence. The estate of being such is productive of those powers of the work which distinguish it from all other sorts of things.

The nonsubstitutability of things may be either circumstantial (as in the silver hammer's case) or integral (as in no reasonable scheme of things is Monet's painting of flowers substitutable for Van Gogh's). Thus the sort of thing a work of affecting presence is—as distinguished from all other sorts of things—a function of the immanence of powers that are integral.

The universe of *means* (rather than of *ends*), whether that which serves as means be either substitutable or nonsubstitutable, is one wholly amenable to reportage or limited reconstitution in language, whether that report be of the thing's status *as thing,* or of the processes in whose execution such a thing might be instrumental. The integral nonsubstitutable, however, defines a separate universe, one to which language bears little relevance. Thus, though language can never reconstitute the analogic, it can cope with it. But when that analogic approaches that integral estate of being replete in the power of end-in-itself, then the adequacies of language are radically diminished. In the work as end, the work's powers are raised to the further power of their ineductable, wholly-otherness.

By so much as we are removed from language and meaning, by so much more, correspondingly, are we moved into affect and import. Affect bears to the nonsubstitutable analogic a relationship similar to that which meaning bears to language: it is the felt part of its synapse, as meaning is the intellectual part of the semantic transaction. The difference, of course, is that in the instance of the word, the relationship to meaning is arbitrary; meaning is not constitutively present in it, its form does not create its meaning. If I say, "It is raining," the words do not have the shape of the event. They have arbitrary shapes and relationships. The word "rain" is neither liquid nor pear-shaped, and it does not execute a downward race by dropping out of syntax, wetting the ear of the listener. On the other hand, in the case of the nonsubstitutable thing, the shapes and processes of that thing are themselves productive of their affect, establishing the consciousness of the witness in precisely those dynamics and qualities initially incarnated into the work as the definitive condition of its being.

The work of affecting presence is distinguished among ordinary things because it is an end-in-itself, and it *is* for one chief, integral reason: namely, that the work is self-constituting. Its self-constitutivity derives from the fact that it is of the nature of a self, owning as its definitive power the necessity of abiding in a condition of self-awareness. This is to say that the work of affecting presence exists in its incarnated consciousness of that which it apperceives. The work *is* the perceived apperceived (though in Suprematism, for example, there are no percepta; only appercepta. Consider Malevich's *White on White*). This is the ontological touchstone of affecting presence. The definitive difference between my photograph of a wheat field, taken in pure literality, and Van Gogh's painting of one lies in the fact that the latter exists in the constitutive condition of Van Gogh's abiding consciousness-of it.

This is the source of the work's subjectivity and the reason the work is a *presence*. As meaning is the product of a proposition, so presence is the yield of the subjectivized analogic. The work is a presence because it is a subject. It is a subject because like man himself, the work is an entity that stands in a state of being conscious-of. If something does not abide in consciousness-of, it misses the necessary condition of its *being* and is but a mere thing.

We may discern two sorts of subjectivized analogic "things." In the first instance there are those which im-mediate directly, for the work of affecting presence does not *mediate* (and does not therefore exist in *media*, but rather in *im-media*, in conditions established *in consciousness-of*). The subjectivized analogic works exist in their own, direct terms, and in these terms are shape-and-dynamic constitutive of what they appear to be (e.g., Rodin's *The Kiss,* or a Mondrian geometrical field). In the second instance, there are those analogic works which proceed to im-mediation by way of mediation, which is to say that they are not, in point of fact, shape-constituted of what is given to the senses *as the apparent terms of their shape-constitution.* I think here of a novel or a verse whose analogicity is not to be found in the type. Such works are constituted through behaviors which do not in and of themselves, in their own terms, constitute what it is that analogically such works are.

Works that proceed through direct im-mediation own a focal point that lies rather more toward the external world; which is to say that such works exist clearly in an external, thingly base. But the focal point of the work which proceeds to im-mediation through mediation (e.g., the poem) tends to lie dead center of the deep self, quickening in sentience. It is an estate and not a thing. One is an art of subjectivized thingliness, of the being of things in the external world; the other is an art of the being of ego, of *estativity.* The former is a pervasion of a work with the presence of self; the latter is the pervasion of a self with a work. The former is a transfiguration of the phenomena of the outer world; the latter is a transfiguration of the inner world. Mystical displacement of the mundane ego is an instance of the transfiguration of the inner world. Naturally, these poles are more readily distinguishable in theory than in practice. Whether a work is one sort or another is, with respect to the power of transfiguration, only a matter of the strength of the tending—whether the force of the transfiguration is toward the out-reaching or, contrariwise, the in-reaching.

Where the inner world—the self—is transfigured, that very apprehension of the self becomes the "subject-matter" (that of which subjectivity is established) of analogicity, so that alternative states of the self's being come to pass within, or in place of, the autobiographically given ones. Because the analogic of alternative selves proceeds to value by way of digital symbols—and hence through meaning—we may say that the analogicity of the self (the self as affecting presence) is brought about because meaning itself constitutes an analogic estate. This is distinguished from other analogic estates by virtue of the fact that language or some other symbol system passes from medium to im-medium. This possibility exists because the symbol system can cue, through a semantic construct, an existential analogicity.

Let us consider the Holy Mass of the Roman Catholic Church as an instance of that digital-analogic which is simultaneously of both meaning and value, both mediative and im-mediative. In the Mass, progress is made via word and act, both of which own symbolic assignations but whose estative values are of more significant moment than their meanings. This is to say, for instance, that the Introit is not really shape-constitutive of an approach to the Holy, but is constitutive of an *estate* of approach. And the elevation of the Host is not in itself factually and objectively constitutive of the presence of Christ; on the contrary, the Christly presence is estatively constitutive of the efficacies of the Host. The focus of the being-in-consciousness-of is within the psyche and not within the external, thingly work.

That work which exists in the Mass—that nonmundane self which is created of the communicant—is the self redeemed through the establishment within the communicant of the indwelling presence of divinity. One can establish a discursive commentary upon the whole Mass; indeed, some of the words of the Mass are themselves discursive upon its own mystery, whereas others are invocative. Yet their meaning exists not only semantically, but existentially as well, for the Mass is not the Mass reposing in type upon the pages of one's missal. The presence of Christ wrought through the offices of the Mass is subjectivized awareness, the estate of divine consciousness-of. This presence informing and transfiguring the communicant is the work.

As phenomenon, a dance of possession is not significantly different with respect to the relation of the visible dimension of the work to its deep realities. Such dancing no more—and no less—than the Mass enacts the necessary and sufficient outer conditions of the interior analogics of redemption. In both cases, the physical acts which define the observable behavior are the triggering devices which effectuate the explosion of self into Grace or God. The outer dimensions of such works are not separable from the inner ones. Words are names of meanings, as gestures are; and meanings themselves are analogic estates of being. The text is the sole condition under which the estate may come to exist. The two are wholly continuous, one with the other. We face here not "formulae," which are shape-descriptive though not shape-constitutive, but rather the visible top of an experience whose totality embraces incredible depths of one's being. We may think of such phenomena as of a class we may call "mediated immediation."

Self-focused works (interior, as opposed to those which are exterior and work-focused) are, perhaps, as ancient as Homo sapiens, and they seem to provide the point of departure into a recent aesthetic phenomenon: as our artists obey their restless cultural imperative of *discovery,* they see that the aesthetic comes for the first time in human experience to be "pure"—devoid of the analogic enactment of familiar items, events, and processes. Works are thus emptied of both "content" and "virtuosity," both of which come to be seen not only as crutches upon which the lame must lean, but also as obstacles to the achievement of an analogics of pure (nonthingly) presentation. Malevich writes, "Visual phenomena of the objective world are, in themselves, meaningless; the significant thing is feeling, as such, quite apart from the environment in which it is called forth." He continues, "Art no longer . . . wishes to illustrate the history of manners, it wants to have nothing further to do with the object, as such, and believes that it can exist in and for itself, without things."[3] In some sense, distinction between artist and scientist becomes blurred, as the fiction of "artistic truth" comes to stand with respect to the soul as inviolably as scientific truth does to the intelligence. In that the analogic is not now (in such movements as Suprematism) of those known forms and workings we encounter (or might encounter) in the world, its center of focus is removed toward the imaginal energies of the consciousness' deep center.

But such art abides not in meanings (in the semantic sense in which

3. Kasimir Malevich, "Suprematism," in *Modern Artists on Art,* p. 93.

I am here using this term), but rather—as is characteristic of the subjectivized analogic—in value. No names are posed. However unfamiliar, that which is executed in consciousness-of is the work itself. Though such works are not *mimetic of* things in the world, yet they *are* things in the world, precisely the same sorts of things that "content" paintings, sculptures, dances, and musical works are. The "content" of works of minimalism, suprematism, abstract expressionism, conceptualism, and so on, is but the analogic of the unfamiliar—of the unknown and, indeed, sometimes even the "unknowable" (in any precise, lexical sense). It is of the universe of objectlessness (an object being that sort of thing of which we may say of it exactly what it is, e.g., a hammer, or a statue, or a composition), melodylessness (a repeatable tune), and situationlessness (a discernible plot). To this universe thingly knowledge is irrelevant. We have in such works a profound revolution in the nature of the powers of thingliness: that which does not exist in our ordinary experience of the world is made to be, suffused with a consciousness-of that is wholly depersonalized (or impersonalized), an "objective" estate of being. This is the universe of the subjectivized objective. We have in such "objectless" works a revolutionary aesthetic achievement, as critical, indeed, as was Homo sapiens' original movement to content-art thirty millennia or so ago.

The literary arts are relevant to this consideration as well—not to the discussion of the nature of "objective" art, but to the nature of the "mediated immediation" of the Mass and the dance of possession. These arts (poetry and narrative) proceed through the employments of the names of meanings to the evocation of subsequent analogic estates. In narrative, the analogic estate evoked is *situation,* whereas in poetry the induced analogic estate is of a lyrical and/or conceptual estate. Of the two, it is only in poetry that language is im-medium; in narrative, language is medium, conveying situation, which is its im-medium. (Indeed the situation can be mimed, for instance, or portrayed in pictures.)

Nearly all prose and all verse exist at points on the continuum between the analogicity of situation and the analogicity of meaning, with "absolute" narration (James Bond novels) being purely situational, in contrast with *Moby Dick* which moves toward poetry, and with narrative poetry being less intensely poetic (less established solely in meaning) than nonsituational, lyric poetry. Narration and poetry, thus, exist in two different sorts of relationships with language; they also exist differently, one from the other, with respect to mediation/im-mediation. Poetry exists more nearly im-mediately in language than does narration—more as the Mass exists, although the parallel is not perfect in that there are important differences as well. For in poetry it is the case that certain physical properties of language (sonal similarities, for example, in rhyme and alliteration, "socialized" forms, such as the sonnet) contribute analogically to the im-mediation of the poetic estate. Further, one may observe that poetry is syndetically achieved (mounting sonal effects, plus patterned rhythmic repetitions, plus certain socialized analogic features, plus the accretion of meanings and ambiguous synapses of meanings), whereas narration is, at base, oppositionally (synthetically) achieved: A has an objective whose realization B thwarts. Clusters of narrational oppositions may exist with respect to each other either syndetically (as in picaresque narratives) or synthetically (as in a Faulkner novel). Similarly, poetry may do so as well, tending toward syndetic emphasis in lyrical poetry and synthetic emphasis in narrative poetry (though *as poetry* always syndetic).

Note the syndesis used in the poetry of an aesthetic of virtuosity. Consider the following stanza from Hart Crane's "Voyages":

> *Take this Sea, whose diapason knells*
> *On scrolls of silver snowy sentences,*
> *The sceptered terror of whose sessions rends*
> *As her demeanors motion well or ill,*
> *All but the pieties of lovers' hands.*[4]

Here we note the syndetic effects of strong alliteration, and of the repetitions of the phonetic brothers t/d. Further, there is a strong accretion—of supplementation—in the unexpected juxtapositions of categories of meanings (e.g., the three-way one of *"scrolls"* of *"silver snowy" "sentences"*). But the focal point of this poem lies not solely in deep-center of self; it tends rather more directly toward the work itself. Meaning is here less exploited for its situational than for its existential analogic, and as much for its physical syndetisms as for its analogicity under the sign of its brilliant semantic edge.

With respect, then, to the subjectivized thingliness of the work of affecting presence, we see a complex continuum from the thing as a work of the world to the thing as a work of the self. It extends from the aesthetic of virtuosity through to the aesthetic of invocation. Any given work, or the works of any given people, may occupy fine points in between: between the

4. Hart Crane, "Voyages," in *The Norton Anthology of Poetry*, p. 1083.

work of pure virtuosity at one extreme (the Rococco), and of pure invocation at the other (the Mass); between the syndetic submission of meaning to being (the icon), and the analogic of the symbolic. Between any two imaginable poles there exist those points that a person, a culture, or an epoch seizes upon and within which it establishes and proclaims being.

Certain of the things-in-power (e.g., a wafer that is later invoked) are sufficiently substitutable (while at the same time partly nonsubstitutable) that they tend toward the category of the thing-as-object almost as much as toward the category of the thing-as-subject. It is also true that some things-as-object tend toward the category of the thing-as-subject so markedly that sometimes they are, in some cultures, called "works of art." I am thinking here of the thing-as-object executed with such virtuosity that it is often held, in some cultures at least (European, American, and Japanese), in the highest esteem. We face here those phenomena we call "crafts." What relationship these craftworks bear to things-as-subject, to the work of affecting presence, has long been of interest to anthropologists. Indeed, such virtuosity of object caused Franz Boas to confound virtuosity with the aesthetic.

If it be the case that a particular public denominates objects of surpassing excellence to be "art," then the integrity of such ethnogenic classification is to be respected, and we are to note that such is the case. But from a perspective outside the culture—which is what we must achieve if we are to make general observations about the nature of things and of man—we must recognize that not everything the public calls "art" is necessarily, therefore, a work of affecting presence.

But however such excellent works be classified within the culture, the fact is that objects of virtuosity are objects nonetheless. The virtuosity of making a horse's shoe does not cause the object to become more than it is; it never analogically constitutes more than the simple condition of being that particular bending and perforation of metal designed to fit to hoof. Nor is the act of shoeing of the same nature as a work of invocation, for it never becomes other than what it is—the forging of a shoe and its subsequent nailing to the hoof. The smith's consciousness-of cannot be said to be incarnate within either shoe or shoeing as a condition of being. No more can either shoe or shoeing be said to be made so as to embody affect, nor can it be defined to be what it is by virtue of the fact that it does so.

The definitive characteristic of works of crafts is that they are task-determined. The pots crafted by a people given to extension and discontinuity are no less round and not necessarily more fit than those of a people contrarily given to intension and continuity. The sewing of a seamstress from a synthetic culture is no less incremental than that of her counterpart from a syndetic culture.

Both object and process of craft are of a sort that whatever might be said about them over and above their objectness (e.g., whether or not they own virtuosity) is to be seen as syndetic enrichment. But not one of such incrementations alters the essence of the objectness of such an object. Whereas a beautifully carved head may crown a heddle pulley, and though this head may in some spiritual sense increment the pulley, still is the object nonetheless a pulley. If an object be shorn of such additives as either power or virtuosity, it is still unambiguously object.

Excellence of manufacture, critical to the work of craft, is as we have already seen irrelevant to the existence of a work of affecting presence in the aesthetic of invocation and in some cases even to the existence of a work of virtuosity (think of those paintings we might regard as "poorly" painted or "badly" designed).

I am not aware that in general usage we ever conceive of the craftswork to be other than spatial. We may speak of a writer, a composer, or a choreographer as being a "fine craftsman," by which we mean that he knows with mastery the full technical ranges of his art. Yet we do not speak of *Oedipus Rex,* or the Beethoven *Missa Solemnis,* or the *Firebird* ballet as being craftsworks.

Finally, because its origin lies in the universal imperative to make useful things (of the substitutable order of things), one cannot say of the craftswork that the relationships it analogically enacts are other than of the nature of those of the class of thing-as-object. The craftswork does not define new relationships, which—constitutively indwelling—give it that presence characteristic of a subject. All this is but a further way of saying that the craftswork is not characterized by a condition of consciousness-of which is ineluctably causative of it.

It is generally the case in human action that the behavioral distance between any two points seems to be infinite, which is to say that between two such different points exist what often seem to be unlimited possibilities of the degree to which any phenomenon might tend toward either the one or the other point. It is thus always difficult and often even impossible toward the middle of the range thus established to determine whether any particular thingly act is object or subject. There is no way to resolve this problem. It is simply the case that the act of such a sort is ambiguous, being at the same time both somewhat of one sort, somewhat of the other.

But of course one passes a point where this particular ambiguity tends to resolve. I think here of certain works of craft which play upon the objectness of the thing-as-object. These are to be seen especially where novelty is highly prized, in an aesthetic of virtuosity. Such works are *based upon* that which is job-oriented. I have in mind here vessels made so that their utility as vessel is wholly invalidated (e.g., is made with holes in it). Such a work relates to vessels in general as a giant Oldenberg icebag does to art in general: it is an extrapolation from the notion of the object, wherein the object is made to bear, as a condition of its being, the artist's awareness of its objectivity. Such works stand between object and subject, but nearer the latter than the former, and nearer the latter than the unambiguous work of craft. The incarnation of powers into thingly existence follows a trajectory from absence of any power save that relating to the achievement of simple analogicity, past the midregion of ambiguous hypostasis and balance, toward the rich incrementation of powers characteristic of the thing-in-presence.

I have been writing of crafts as of the virtuosity of things-as-objects. But implicit in all I have said so far is a notion of the thing-as-object as an item owning a clear quality of thingliness in the world, helping to fulfill man's roles or his needs abroad in that world. But there is a further kind of thing-as-object whose efficacy exists not with respect to operations upon the world, but rather with respect to operations upon the self and upon the environment that self psychologically inhabits. As the thing-as-object ranges from that which is without virtuosity to that to which virtuosity is a syndetic addition, so does the thing-as-object-of-self similarly range with respect to vituosity. *Craft* can thus be seen as applying to both the object-of-the-world and the object-of-self when executed with the enrichment of virtuosity.

These objects-of-self are those pieces and colors with which we decorate both our bodies and the spaces of our domestic and public worlds (excluding, of course, works of affecting presence), and those sounds, movements, and "rites" with which we amuse our selves in the dimensions of our time. This class of decorative and entertaining things, so multitudinously prevalent in the contemporary world, I name the world of "decortainment."

It includes jewelry, toys, games, social dances, variety shows, plastic busts of presidents, plaster vases, cocktail parties, many pop tunes, and movies—all of which may be said to be things but lightly touched with subjectivity. Because they are not defined by the incarnation of consciousness-of or by the presence of indwelling value and seriousness or probity, the things of decortainment are often nothing more than temporal or spatial trinkets. But they are nothing less, either, and if we are to understand the thingly excrescences of man's consciousness, we must not fail to consider its decorative manifestations.

It is important to bear in mind that pieces of decortainment are always syndetically employed. They are properties in the additive creation of the self as an affecting work, a process most notable (when they are important pieces) in the establishment of a priest, a warrior, or a king. When the self is presented in the syndetism of items rich with power, the self is a work of invocation. But when such pieces are either merely remarkable or negligible, then the product is the establishment of a work of virtuosity.

The analogic is not only shape-constitutive; it is also of that roundedness —that free-standingness—that in physically analogic objects we call "three-dimensionality." This is to say that all analogic things own a sense of midpoint and of fullness from midpoint simultaneously toward both front and back, toward sides, and toward top and bottom as well. In the dimensions of time, the similetic equivalent of the midplane is the present that roots in the past and portends toward the future. Each analogic point in lived time and space, therefore, exists in that estate the photographer calls "depth-of-field." When an analogic thing (be it spatial, temporal, or imaginal—as literary works) is focused upon by the intention of consciousness, it emerges into clarity of depth-of-field, its context tending to blur toward the edges, so creating that temporal or spatial echoing we call "ambiguity."

Whereas in the case of the broadly, interclass substitutive analogic (a heel or a hammer) this ambiguity is not present with import, it is necessarily so in the work of affecting presence, creating a nimbus of dim, diffused, peripheral intentions within which the work stands forth in bright clarity. The radiance of a work is a function of the fineness, precision, and pervasion of the consciousness' apperception thereof.

In space we perceive three-dimensionality because of our stereoptical ability. In time, however, we experience the significant moment because of our historicity, for we know that moment only in the redolence of the past and the augmentations or diminutions the future seems to promise. Alternatively, we may, as in mystical rapture, know the felt-present upon that axis established between it and timelessness.

Each analogic point fixed by our consciousness exists, therefore, in "stereo"—stereotemporally, stereospatially, stereoptically, stereosituationally, and so on. At least two points must be established either simultaneously or successively, in order that "perspective" of apprehension might be achieved in requisite depth-of-field. Thus, in a novel, we apperceive any particular action of the protagonist simultaneously in terms of what he has done or what he is about to do; or an instant in music, as a point deriving from what has gone before and leading to involvements and resolutions whose precise nature we know not but whose general direction we intuit. Van Gogh's wheat field abides between that which is not the painting (the wall upon which it hangs, the memory of the wheat field one saw driving through Nebraska) and that which is *as apperceived by the artist;* between the golden color of natural wheat, and the golden which in Van Gogh's work flows through the field like blood; between the nature of ordinary perception and the nature of aesthetic perception; between the two mythologemic energies of fertility and self, and so on until such a point of wholeness is reached that the work springs forth into being.

If I perceive an ancestor figure (and am of congruent belief), I perceive it as between spirit of tree and spirit of ancestor; as among syndetism and intension and continuity; as between form (syndetic intension) and "content"; between belief in ancestors and belief in the possibility of their invocation. If I perceive it in terms of my own aesthetic, I apprehend it as between excellence and mediocrity, between gestalt and traits, and so on.

We see the same movement in the semantic analogic (metaphor). Here the analogic subjectivity (the unique act of the work's intending) is achieved through the simultaneous, mutual positing of two or more terms. But if this configuration of stereosystems so multifariously endows the work with depth-of-subjectivity (of complex intentions incarnate in the work as that consciousness-of within which it abides), that presence is its eventuation. It is the stereomythicity of the work—penumbrations of the general consciousness of our kind—which most deeply incarnates it in power. The work's givenness in that ambiguity which exists between its clarity and the blurredness of its context is such that it derives further, though more obscure, powers therefrom. These powers of ambiguity are not a portion of the work's consciousness-of, but rather are—however inextricable it may be from them—peripheral, ancillary attendant and not incarnate. This, then, is to be seen as a further stereoreality of the work of affecting presence.

On the one hand man has through time acted in certain sorts of general ways —organizing his life with respect to others, using language, worshipping gods, and so on. This is a consciousness all men share. On the other hand, the degree of freedom permitted man has been such that he has, through history and across space, defined numerous different styles of life we call "cultures." What is true of such institutionalized behaviors is similarly true of his thingly behavior: *making things* is not only culturally characteristic in respect of technique, style, etc.; it is also a generic act characteristic of all men. Receptacles are common to all men, as are strings to bind with, and tools, and weapons, and domiciles. Making things, making institutions, making both of these under some circumstances the bearers of myth—all these processes enact power. These are the deep powers of man, his "vertical" powers, and together with one's unique history as an individual they constitute that dimension of the consciousness we may call the "diaconsciousness" (the diachronic consciousness). The individual particularities of this diaconsciousness, in cross-sectional configuration at any instant in one's life, are to be generalized under the name of the "synconsciousness" (the synchronic consciousness). Every individual, if a wholly functioning entity, lives at the point where these two aspects of consciousness intersect.

The diaconsciousness' complexity is suggested by the extremes I have already indicated: everything in between man's species imperatives—those toward language, social organization, etc.—and his myths, and down to the memories of his individual experiences. How deeply into the recesses of his biological existence reach the roots of his consciousness is not difficult to say: they are coterminous. Thus there are determinants upon man's consciousness deriving from the fact that he is an animal rather than a plant, a vertebrate rather than an invertebrate, and so on. Whatever the case in this respect, we must expect that these orders of the diaconsciousness, being common to all men, inhere in the conditions of our being Homo sapiens.

Human consciousness is characterized by stability and change—by a strong determination toward the conservation of ancient conditions of awareness and estates of being, and at the same time by such experimentation as may, in vastitudes of time, lead to further species innovations. The problem of the thing, and ultimately of the nature of works of affecting presence, is thus a problem of both the diaconsciousness and the syncon-sciousness. With respect to works of affecting presence, we see that works tending primarily toward the diaconsciousness are to be perceived as strongly "mythopoetic" (which is to say forthrightly celebrating the mytho-formal and the mythologemic), while those primarily celebrating the syn-consciousness, pushing the strong energies of the diaconsciousness to the background, are "idiopoetic." The mythopoetic is more pervasively charac-teristic of the works of a culture of invocation, whereas the idiopoetic is characteristic of a culture of the aesthetic of virtuosity.

Powers enliven all those particularities thought by the people of a given culture to own affecting presence. These powers are numerous and hierar-chical: the power of externalized purpose, affect-attended; the power of the analogic, or making things which are self-definitive and shape- and process-constitutive; the power of the nonsubstitutive; and the power of relational-ity, binding man through works of incarnated presence into relationships with the powers of the divine and the beautiful. But primary among all these is the power of subjectivity of standing-in-consciousness-of, even as a human person does.

This immediative and entelechous relationship perpetrated in the world by the work of affecting presence exists in a special and further estate of thingly power, that of subjectivity. This power of self-reflectivity may derive from the subjectivity of the individual creator (as in a Rembrandt), the culture (as in a generic mask, e.g., the Yoruba Gelede), or a god (as in the Mass or in a dance of possession). This power of subjectivization can be brought into being through a self's holding in the powers of witnessing a spatial work (painting, sculpture, building), or a temporal one (music, narrative, verse), or such works as are both at the same time (dance). It can exist in the world or be centered in the psyche.

The thing-in-power—the work of affecting presence—is first a thing, a *thing relationshipping.* We must bear in mind the ineptitude of language for coping with the analogic, lest we perhaps innocently try to skew the nature of the thing which is asemantic to that which language can adequately formulate. Bateson's observation concerning the nature of dolphin language —that it may perhaps be a digital system whose content is analogic[5]— suggests the dolphins' language could more adequately than man's come to

5. Bateson, "Cetacean Communication," p. 374.

grips with the thingly world. There is little evidence, however, either that we are to understand that language or that the dolphin is about to become interested in art. However, the invention of such a language is imperative if we are greatly to expand our "understanding" of art. If we could develop a language of qualities and of wholeness of relationships and of affect that is as adroit and subtle as that which has over the centuries been invented by mathematicians, then we should be positioned adequately and appropriately to speak of the thingly world, embracing the works of affecting presence. Meanwhile we must continue to explore, bearing our limitations in mind and pointing—however inadequately, but as perceptively and as truly as we can—to some of the definitive and constitutive features of such phenomena. Most of all, we must avoid the error of confounding affect with meaning, the work with the item, presence with symbol, and art with language.

In sum, the definitive power of works of affecting presence is subjectivity, the power of the work's standing in a state of consciousness-of. That abiding in affective apperception-of is a special estate of relating self to world, such that the value which in *thing* merely *attends* is freed and made incarnate and causative, with the result that the work tends to become end rather than only means.

The powers of the analogic are various, and range in kind and order from those of the simplest occurrences of "body language" to those of the most majestic monuments of affecting presence. And the powers accrue, so that in the external analogic lie the powers of those shared with the body analogics of other animals. And relationality endures in subjectivity, and subjectivity abides in the mythic—all the way to the power of the excitement of the individual work. Moreover, the work abides in the further power of ambiguity, for it prevails as a bonding of thing and more-than-thing, of object and subject, physical and cognitive, the perceptible and the apperceptible. In the invoked work the ambiguity is syndetically interpreted: the thing is at one time merely object and at another time wholly suffused with subjectivity. In the work of virtuosity, the work is forever both at the same time, resolving for us sometimes with mildness of affect but at other time with the radiance of transcendent subjectivity. All the powers I have discussed in this chapter are ontological powers, and the deep presence they yield are the work's ontological presence. One calls these powers "ontological" because they are the definitive powers of the work of affecting presence as such—irrespective of kind of aesthetic, cultural or epochal provenience, or identity of content. This is not true of those powers that shall follow in our consideration, for these subsequent powers are substantively optative and culturally selective. What I mean by these two assertions will become clear in the following chapters.

Perhaps we might mention some of those fixed apperceptions which, incarnating within a work, cause it to bear that subjectivity—that standing-in-apperception of—definitive of the work of affecting presence. For this purpose, I shall discuss the Gelede dancing of the Yoruba people.[6]

Gelede is one of the names of the great Mother goddess, also known as *Iyanla* and *Onile*. As *Onile*, her aspect as earth goddess is stressed, while as the other two her role as controller of the *aje*, or witches, is emphasized. The *aje* are creatures who personify certain of her feminine powers—most particularly those relating to human fertility. Thus the *aje*, unlike the Western witch, may be either "good" or "bad." Perhaps even these terms do not appropriately describe the activities of the *aje*. It may be best simply to say that the *aje* work the powers of the goddess, and that sometimes these appear to be "evil," while at other times they appear to be "good."

The ambiguity attending the *aje* is further suggested by the fact that they are quite as likely to be called "mothers" as anything else. The use of this term seems to suggest the generalization of their power, for all women, as controllers of fertility (as is seen to be the case), are affiliated with *Gelede*. Further, it is a woman past the age of fertility—thus existing in a special relationship with the powers of the goddess—who is her priestess and who presides over the annual Gelede festival of which the Gelede dance is an important part. The function of this annual festival is to honor and delight the goddess, her priestess *(Iyalashe)*, and the women and mothers. The benefit aspired to is fertility of womb and earth. (The ceremony is sometimes specially held to help some woman become fertile or to encourage a safe delivery by one who has in the past given birth with great difficulty.)

At a time immediately prior to the festival—the auspiciousness of whose date has been previously ascertained through divination—the masks are brought before *Iyalashe* for blessing, sacrifice (they are offered food), and the renewal of their color, which makes them look young and strong. (Rob-

6. Peggy Harper, "The Role of Dance in the Gelede Ceremonies of the Village of Ijio," pp. 67–94.

ert Farris Thompson has shown the necessity of "ephebism"—of portraying the figure or the mask at the height of young maturity and strength.[7])

When the time of the festival comes to pass, songs are sung, prayers are offered, and finally the female mask appears to dance in preparation for the appearance of the *Efe* mask. At this point some ambiguity exists, for although the *Efe* seems to be a male mask, it seems to be female as well (e.g., the delicacy of its face). The *Efe* is the ritually most powerful and most sacred of the various masks, most of which, however, have similar faces (see plates 5–8). The *Efe* dancer is robed in layer upon layer of skirts and panels, so that great bulk is built up—suggesting a plentitude or a pregnancy appropriate to the goddess—and so that in the turns of the *Efe* dancer the various panels lend a syndetic complexity to the visual events in the space of the dancer's turning and twirling. Indeed, the multilayered costume enacts this dynamic of syndetism even when the dancer is at rest.

After the first—tentative and awesome—appearance of the *Efe* dancer, the sacral intensity of the dance becomes gradually ameliorated, first as *Efe* himself dances, then as paired female dancers (danced in fact by young men—a further syndetism of ambiguity) execute enormously complex spatial replications of the temporal syndetisms of the drumming. Finally, the "female" dancers are replaced by a pair of dancers masked as buffaloes, who seem to be wholly for amusement. The total dance-in-time is characterized by a structurally syndetic fullness of lesser syndetisms (e.g., individual dances, music, costuming) in which the "parts" of the dance exist accretively and not through internal entailments (though they may be "entailed" by the external requirements of tradition).

The work's incessant syndetisms constantly enact the subjectivity of fulfilling the primal processes of supplementation which characterize the Yoruba apperception of the world. Further, the dance is executed in the fullness of the presence of the spirit of *Gelede,* who is both observer *(Iyalashe)* and the observed *(Efe)*—indwelling the whole dance ceremony, endowing it with that divine subjectivity whose presence will enrich both womb and earth.

The *Gelede* subjectivity is further intensified by the work's *relating,* for bringing consciousness into being as projected in the intimate relationships of cognition lies at the essence of the subjectivity of both person and work. Thus we see warm femininity held in the grip of the chilling possibilities

7. Robert Farris Thompson, *Black Gods and Kings: Yoruba Art at UCLA,* ch. 3/3.

of infertility, intimacy in the threat of the unknown, man held in thrall by gods, and gods made visible among men. Against a background of rich beliefs and complex attitudes toward witches, we sense their imminence, and the occasional holds the eternal in its transitory grip, just as the general does the particular, and the social the individual. These tensions are but a few of the twinges of consciousness which bring the *Gelede* into the vitality of affecting presence, which deliver into fertility the threatening barrenness of seasons.

3

THE POWERS OF
THE MYTHOLOGEMIC

The stories of Pygmalion and Galatea, and of Tar Baby are parables about the nature of the work of affecting presence. Both recognize the fact that between the life of a man and the "life" characteristic of the work there exists a closeness of kind so marked that under certain circumstances one seems to pass over into the other. Both stories are ways of coming to terms with that essential subjectivity whose establishment within the work endows it with affecting presence.

It is Galatea and Tar Baby themselves who first command our interest. In both of these "sculptures" the work's subjectivity is freed from that oneness of the consciousness' attention characteristic of aesthetic phenomena, and released to that universal fixability of apperception characteristic of the consciousness of the human person. Servitude to one apperception thus having been demolished, the two created works become free agents.

This helps us somewhat understand the nature of that relationship in the work of affecting presence between the apperceived and the process of its apperception—from which, to be sure, it is inalienable. It is the fixity of the power of *thing* (the analogic) held in the power of value and affect —of subjectivity—which is definitive of the particular kind of subjectivity the work owns. In brief, subjectivity is a function of relationships between the insentient and the sentient, the thing and the person. Even as in the literary metaphor, where the power of one word is held in the power of the field of another, so is the aesthetic phenomenon to be seen in its most general aspect as the power of one estate enacted under the power of another —the power of the analogic held in the field of the power of subjectivity. The work thus exists as a binding together of different universes, each holding the other in field. As the corpus callosum exists between the hemispheres of the brain, bringing their somewhat different but complementary functions into the power of the "three-dimensionality" appropriate to our experience of reality, so does the work of affecting presence bind together into "stereopticality" both objectivity and subjectivity.

This narrative recognition of the nature of the work's subjectivity (Galatea and Tar Baby) occurs variously among the world's peoples. Indeed, we see it emerge in different forms and at various times in our own Western culture. Thus we have the story in negative aspect in the tale of Frankenstein's monster (where if the monster is not a "work of art," at least it is a "made person"), and we encounter it more pleasantly in Tchaikovsky's *Nutcracker* and in the ballet *Coppelia.* A more homely tale gives it to us in the gingerbread man. And so on. The Yorubas' neighbors tell the story in reverse: they often believe that the Yoruba capture the children of other people, transforming them into automatons whose chief function is to vomit money. It is rather suggestive of the Hansel and Gretel legend where the reverse Galatea process is also invoked.

The fact that such tales exist suggests that the work's subjectivity participates in that generality of acknowledgment we think of as *myth,* which is a special font of aesthetic power. It would be erroneous to presume, however, that the mythic with its attendant power is restricted to the universe of affecting presence. We are as likely to encounter the mythic in government as in art; in fact in some instances, such as the person of a mighty king, distinctions between the two become tenuous. Indeed, it need not be as person that the mythic appears. It may as easily be a situation: "boy meets girl," in vulgar parlance; more eruditely, "the good child and the bad." It may be neither of these, but it may be a process (such as dramatic *eventuation,* or the installation of a king); a dynamic (such as crescendo or diminuendo); a place (a palace, a temple, a sacred cave or grove); or a thing (a ring, a crown, a sword).

The mythic is the universe of our consciousness' enactment of certain general, highly abstract, universal, and generative dynamics of being human. The manifestations of the mythic, of all the other sources of power we have thus far mentioned—facticity, analogicity, subjectivity—are the most explicitly known to us. Thus it is with a shock of recognition that those of us who know Galatea recognize Tar Baby, or that the Anyi maternity sculpture (plate 9) is as touching to us as a Raphael Madonna and Child.

These universal, generative energies and states are "mythologems" (a word I borrow from Jung, who uses it to mean "archetype"), and they occur in fairly stable form from people to people. There is a further dimension to the mythic, however, whose powers subjectivize the work: that of cultural particularities exercised either upon these mythologems in full potency or in ameliorated energy. Thus it is important for us to note that in the cases of both Pygmalion and Tar Baby, we have evidence of the clear influences of their begetting cultures. For it is a fact that as there are general mythic classes whose members flash through our beings, so are there cultural determinants to the mythic. So do we see in the one instance (Pygmalion) that the created work is brought into life because its smitten creator wishes it to be; and that in the second instance there seems to be less interest in the stories as to *how* the life of the created thing comes about than in the fact that such is indeed the case. In the first instance, the created thing is brought into life by virtue of an oppositional relationship between a woman-hater (Pygmalion) and the goddess of love (Aphrodite). Galatea's quickening is a function of the unnatural state of affairs existing between the two of them, and in the long run is its resolution. Further, creator and creature wed and produce children. In the second case, Tar Baby (and it should be noted that "Tar Baby" identifies a—syndetic—corpus of many tales concerning the creature) simply goes from one involvement to another, through his stickiness universally accreting to himself various of the world's things and inhabitants. Both processes exist as systems of relationships—synthetic in Pygmalion and Galatea, syndetic in Tar Baby.

Syndesis and synthesis are themselves mythologemic, and the former is, as we have seen, "prior to" the latter in that the powers it exercises tend to be universal among the peoples of humankind, whereas those of the latter do not. I define "mythologems" as those universal and enduring configurations of the consciousness (efflorescent and recognized in the synconsciousness, but rooted to the deepest recesses of the diaconscious' analogic powers) of content, conformation, and process which have become specific (i.e., "of the species") and recurring themes in man's enactment of self and world. Thus a universal narrative gem such as "the good child and the bad" is also mythologemic, as are the relatively greater-than-normal size accorded the head in much of "primitive" sculpture, and the movement of the body with the music's beat (rather than *off* the beat, although off-beat movement may be mythologemic as well). The appearance of the mythic as "tales" in language is only its most obvious manifestation, not its sole one —not even its most important one. It is only because the mythic is more readily identifiable in words that we have tended to confound the study of the mythic with the study of verbal myths, a limitation from which we must extricate ourselves and our learning if we are to understand either myth or man. This was a limitation well known to Carl G. Jung, whose great contribution to human understanding lies in escape into the perception and recognition of the many and alternative faces and physiologies of the mythic.

Whereas the mythoform is a culturally specific dynamic of time-space-process, the mythologems are certain thematic and dynamic nodules of consciousness which exist recurringly and powerfully among man's behavioral options, those from among which man selects the points which eventuate into religions, myth-tales, monuments, rituals, much of the art—the whole range of his affective behavior. The mythologems are equally available to all men. As the mythoform is the power of man's cultural construction of the world, the mythologems are the powers of the primal points of his humanity, those insisting upon the recognition, in a power of feeling, of signal achievements in the human consciousness. Mythologems are eidetic monuments, original and immemorial coalescences of the energies of being human. They can be either the cognized or the cognizer—the subject (or theme) of affecting presence or the subjectivizer in whose mighty field the cognized is held in fee. The mythologems are as given as institutional imperatives—kingship, priesthood—both of which are mythologemic.

In the culture of the aesthetic of invocation, the mythologemic is more likely to be enacted plenteously and forthrightly in works of affecting presence than in the aesthetic of virtuosity, which, with its ardent individualism, tends to obscure the general beneath the details of the particular. In the aesthetic of invocation, the ancestor, the messenger of the gods, the creator god—all mythologemic roles—stand forth in mythologemic purity. Their enactments are socialized, their generality little ameliorated with biographical particularities. It is only in the cultures of the aesthetic of virtuosity that the demand is so great for freshness of expression that the mythologemic declares itself in the idioms of individual particularity. It is here that the hermeneutics of critics are required to suggest to us what, in more primal cultures, is immediately available to all. In these latter cultures, works are known in terms of their generalities. When a Yoruba priest for Shango, the thunder god, dances in honor of his god, he carries a figured implement (plates 10–14) invariably bifurcating into twin blades (celts). The *figure* is not causative of the piece's power; the *doubleness* is. One can see numerous variations in the figuration of these pieces. Indeed, there need not be any figures at all; the presence of blades alone is sufficient. Double mythologemic themes are invoked here: the beliefs among the Yoruba that the operative principle of a thunderbolt is a wedge-shaped stone celt, which is of the essence of Shango's power, and that the principle of two-ness is powerful in itself. Twins are of special importance to Thundergod Shango, and the significance of such speciality can be understood only against the background realization of the particular importance twins have for all Yoruba. This in turn can be appreciated only against the recognition of the primal importance of syndesis to the Yoruba. And so it goes. The mythologemic presentation of the Shango dance wand becomes multiple—power after power syndetically established and revealed to us as we successively penetrate the various levels of presentation.

One knows the mythoform "in his bones" as a rightness or a wrongness of the world. If one were to speak by analogy, one might then say that whereas the mythoform is the particular gearings which dictate the mechanics of the expenditure of the energies of consciousness, the mythologems are the parts through which the possibilities of gearing are realized.

The power of mythologems is to be found in their ability to raise each of us from the awful isolation of singularity toward kind-liness. This is more clearly seen in some of the works of the Yoruba, for instance, than in the majority of twentieth-century American works. The Gelede masks (plates 5–8) danced in honor of the powers of the mothers-witches and the masks of Egungun (plates 15, 16), which honor the generic powers of the ancestors, each of which transmutes individuals into instances of the general. Yorubaness is achieved through the powers of the mythoform, but humanity is achieved through the act of articulating the person upon a far profounder point: the mythologemic stillpoint of the turning of our kind. That which subsumes us invests us—and our works—with the power of that very action. That which subsumes us may be a nation (or its paraphernalia—flag or president), a god, a mask of the ancestors, or Paleolithic paintings. The mythologemic is the universe of such generalities.

Both the mythologems and the mythoforms are fonts of power, and in every work both powers are copresent, one flowing into the other, merging into a common pool from which the work draws the sustenance of its own presence. The mythoformal is but the particular and culturally specific apportionment and configuration of certain of the mythologemic powers, a configuration especially powerful to the culture it energizes, because through it the people of that culture construe and live their world. Thus, intension, continuity, and syndesis are each mythologems, whereas their particular degree and intensity of association, their quality and balance into the Yoruba "formula," for example, are culturally unique, the necessary and sufficient condition of *being Yoruba.* Mythoformal, in short.

Mythologems, I have already said, are of more sorts than the substantive. They are powers of estates, powers of relationships, powers of process, powers of occasion, powers of place, powers of pace, and powers of space, time, and dynamic. Further, concerning the substantive powers, one must say that they are of two sorts: powers of person and powers of theme. Although any formal discussion of the mythologems would require a magnitude of treatment quite beyond our space—and our needs—here, it is nevertheless both possible and desirable to touch briefly upon them.

1. POWERS OF ESTATES   Here I have in mind estates of the psyche which obtain in really remarkably similar fashions from culture to culture. (Indeed, this criterion holds for all of the mythologems I shall discuss, and so is to be considered a mythologemic hallmark.) I think of three sorts as examples: possession, socially transitional—or "liminal"—estates, and madness.

a) Possession. Possession is, of course, an estate of affecting presence in which a god or spirit indwells a mortal body, transforming ordinary behavior and altering basic metabolic functions (speeding the heartbeat, fluttering the eyes, "frothing" the mouth). In a Yoruba work of danced affecting presence honoring certain gods, the god's taking—"riding"—of a dancer's body defines the high point of presence. Vision quests of some of the American Plains Indians were conducted under circumstances of great physical deprivation and endurance, so that normal metabolic activities were weakened and a displacement of the ordinary personality was brought about—most desirably so that the self was usurped and indeed displaced by the presence of a totemic animal who thereafter was one's spiritual familiar, guide, and master, one toward whom he stood in a relationship of awful responsibility.

b) Socially transitional estates. Perhaps one most readily thinks here of those universally critical estates—puberty, marriage, and death. All cultures mark them, usually by *rites de passage,* which are themselves enacted works in which the *presence* is brought about through the invoked coming-into-being of the new estate. Circumcision yields the circumcised, analogically present; the marriage, by whatever procedures blessed, once invoked is thereafter (according to culturally variable terms) an existential reality. In syndetic cultures (or insofar as a culture is syndetic), death tends to mark but the end of one phase of mortality and the onset of one more of such liminal phases—as among the Yoruba, where death yields a rest between incarnations.

c) Madness. Madness is common in human culture, and it bears a close relationship with the creation of the work of affecting presence. Plato notes poetry to be a kind of "divine madness." My own inquiry reveals that the people of the Yoruba city of Oshogbo sometimes regard the artists who live there as "quite mad." I should note at this point the peculiarly syndetic mythoformal treatment of madness among the Yoruba: multiple tiny incisions, in regular, parallel rows, are cut into the scalp of the mad individual. The mythoform is enacted in order to bring about a cure.

2. POWERS OF RELATIONSHIPS   Mythologemic relationships are not, generically, necessarily linguistic ones. Rather, they tend to be both analogic and existential. They are, thus, primarily enacted, and but secondarily *asserted.* I think of begettor/begotten (which is perhaps the most elementary of all relationships), more distal versions of which are cause/effect, lesser/greater, giving/receiving.

In the work of affecting presence, a paradox comes to exist with respect to begettor/begotten, for although the creator of the work is its begettor—and it, in turn, his begotten—yet once the work has come into being it reverses the order of this relationship, becoming in its turn his begettor. This is the richest possible kind of relationship, invoking also the relationship between culture and person, god and believer, ancestor and descendant, and (peculiarly to the work in an aesthetic of virtuosity) excellence of perceptibles and magnitude of the power of effect.

Lesser/greater also names the relationship of man to gods, of individual to ancestor, or of the needful to plenitude, all of which are enacted in the work of invocation. Despite the fact of its co-occurrence with begettor/begotten, the relationship of lesser/greater must not be confounded with it, for the latter is of the nature of cause/effect, whereas the former is of part/whole.

Giving/receiving is a most powerfully enacted mythologem in the invoked work of affecting presence where it is (through the offices of sacrifice) a mediated relationship between work and person: the devotee "gifts" the work which in turn "gifts" him. In the work of the aesthetic of virtuosity, in contrast with the invoked work where that which is given is of a different nature from that which is received (i.e., blood is given, increase received), that which is given (virtuosity of creation) is the precise other half of that which is received (virtuosity of affect).

3. POWERS OF PROCESS   The generation and transferability of essence is the primary process of affecting presence, whether in the aesthetic of invocation or, alternatively, in the aesthetic of virtuosity. In the former this invoked donational mythologem is enacted in the various increments of power essences made to the work's item, each increment endowing the item with its own essence, toward the end of enriching the item, toward the end of transmuting it into work. In the case of the work of the aesthetic of virtuosity, essence is the distillate of virtuosity and is maintained in the degree and character of its initial power so long as the work endures.

4. POWERS OF OCCASION   In Yorubaland, Ifa divination reveals whether the gods approve the time for a ceremony—Gelede, for example. If Ifa agrees with a proposed date, the Gelede is danced on a mythologemically propitious occasion, the divine approval of the day constituting a dimension of the *Gesamtkunstwerk's* presence. Professor Henry Glassie tells me that in Ireland the great significance attached to St. Patrick's Day derives as much from the fact that it occurs in the middle of the spring season as from the fact that it is an important saint's day (midposition owning great significance in Irish spatiotemporal values). Solstices are examples par excellence of the power of occasion.

5. POWERS OF PLACE   There is a power to certain places, natural or man-made. Thus, concerning the latter, palace or temple enacts the myths of time, space, and dynamic (see pp. 86–88). But natural places often possess (or are possessed of) mythologemic powers as well. Sacred groves abound in Yorubaland. And I have already mentioned the crossroad, a spot widely held to be of special significance, one we here recognize as mythologemic in its power to abide in disquietude. The fact that in Yoruba the crossroad is sometimes marked by a shrine to Eshu, god of indeterminacy, is as strong a testimony as is the fact that in rural Europe the crossroad was sometimes marked with a crucifix.

6. POWERS OF PACE   However it is culturally interpreted, the change from slow to fast—or from fast to slow—seems to possess mythologemic power. There are at least some instances in which Yoruba possession can occur only under the power of the mounting fastness of music and dance. In European

cultures, we tend to equate slow pace with solemnity, such that the power of dignity abides in slow and stately progress.

7, 8, 9. POWERS OF SPACE, TIME, DYNAMIC If an object or an event extends in space or time, tending toward the fullest of any possible exploitation of physical or fanciful dimensions, or of complexity, this extension is the enactment of a mythologem. Similarly, if it intends, seeking center in all these respects, then it also enacts a mythologem—alternative but, withal, more universal and doubtless more ancient than the one that extends. If an object or event is so construed that the strongest definition is accorded the comprising parts, in their richness as parts, emphasizing boundaries and the molecular nature thereof, then that object or event is discontinuous and mythologemic; so too is it continuous and mythologemic in the opposite case. Similarly, syndesis is mythologemic, as is synthesis. As intension is more primal than extension, so are continuity and syndesis more primal than their mythologemic alternatives.

Cultural mythologemic option (mythoform) may be for any point along these various continua. Thus the Yoruba embrace lateral intension in their sculptures, but emphasize breasts in female figures, thus suggesting a tendency toward ventral extension. However, the overriding affect is toward intension. The Yoruba also stress continuity and syndesis.[1]

10. POWER OF PERSON Mythologems of person are more numerous than those of any category I have thus far mentioned. I shall name but several: creator god (Yoruba Olorun), twins (see Yoruba ibejis), wise old men (ancestor figures), artifice (Ogun, Yoruba god of iron), and the artist.

11. POWER OF THEME Good over evil, evil over good; birth, death, and resurrection—such are themes, vast generative energies whose powers are among the most common of the human psyche. One suspects that themes are the categories of human being. The purer their invocation, which is to say the less biographical and particular they are, the more powerful they tend to be. This is why socialized art, tending to be more general than does highly individualized art, seems more vigorously, more awesomely to move.

Mythologems are universal properties of human consciousness. They are *given* human behavior, and they are as definitive of Homo sapiens as a spinal column is of phylum Chordata. But as the prevalence of marked diversities

1. I devote ample discussion to these points not only in this work, but also in my two previous books, *The Affecting Presence* (1971) and *Wellspring* (1975).

of human cultural—and, within that, individual—behavior reveals, man's realization of his species-defined behavior is optional as to enactment or nonenactment of any particular option, or as to the precise point of enactment on a continuum between fulfillment and nonfulfillment thereof, and as to the intensity or magnitude of such enactment.

The chief characteristic of the mythologem, beyond its universality, is its peculiar strength and fecundity in the consciousness. Jung characterizes it as being *energy*. Further, the mythologem is (of the two universes I previously discussed) analogic rather than digital, a condition which follows directly from the fact that *energy*—or *power*—is itself analogic, which is to say that its characteristics are constitutive of it rather than merely arbitrary (as a word is of a meaning).

The mythologemic powers of the human consciousness are primary. They inform the consciousness independently of the work of affecting presence in one way, whereas in the work of affecting presence they inform it in yet another fashion. In the first instance they refract into the countless details of daily, pragmatic living; in the latter they exist in a state of invocation (in the aesthetic of virtuosity as well as in the aesthetic of invocation), such that they approach the point of filling the available aesthetic "space" in their own terms.

The universal distribution of mythologemic energies—however many of them might be realized in any particular culture—argues that they are as inherent an inevitability in the processes of the enactment of the consciousness as is the eventuation of language, social organization, and other institutions. Thus we see these paradigms fulfilling themselves as readily and as pervasively in Euro-American culture as we do in that of the Yoruba. Let me call attention to some of these in rapid account, *italicizing* the mythologems. In Roman Catholicism, for instance—as it is practiced by its most devout *followers*—*godhead* is divided into three *persons*, two of whom are *creators* (Jehovah and the Holy Ghost), while the other is both a *sustainer* (gives salvation) and is of *extraordinary birth*. Further, in Christianity, the ranks of the *sustainers* swell—not only is there Jesus, but also the choirs of the *angels*, the communion of the *saints*.

We even encounter the subcategories of *elemental gods* (the Holy Ghost appears in *fire*, and God "bids the mighty *ocean* deep / its own appointed limits keep"). The Blessed *Virgin* fulfills general *mother* functions; *ancestors* survive in that selective ancestor worship represented by the saints; the Holy Spirit is the *initiator*; Saint Michael the Archangel is the *protector*; Satan is the *destroyer*. Christianity may be monotheistic, but it is clearly polymyth-ologemic.

The Yoruba similarly reveal a wide exploitation of *gods* and *heroes*. Olorun is the *supreme god, ruler* of earth and sky, *begetter* of all. Excepting the creation of souls, which is Olorun's work, the actual acts of creation are done by lesser gods. Thus Obatala *creates* land, and Odudua creates man. Of the elemental gods, Onile is *goddess of earth and fertility*, Oko is *god of planting* and agriculture, and Olorun under his aspect of Oba-Orun is *king of the sky*. Shango is *thunder god*. And although Olokun is *god of the sea*, each river has its deity. Onile is not the only *mother goddess*; so are Gelede and Oya. Gelede is also *mother of mystery*—and in some sense of evil as well, being mother of witches. *Ancestors* are plentiful, and are to be thought of as *father* mythologems—especially the male ancestors of the Oro society. The *initiators* are many; more frequently than not, they are tribal elders rather than gods, though the elders stand in approach of that deific estate of ancestors. Certainly Eshu (plates 17, 18) is the great *transformer, master of ambiguity, presider over crossroads*, incarnation of uncertainty. Ifa, complementarily, is *god of certainty*, and thus a *protector god*. Although no god destroys, there are the witches who, in addition to perpetrating other evils upon humans, can also *eat men's souls*. *Twins, albinos*, and *dwarfs* are powerful, and *composite creatures* abound; so do changeable ones, in that witches characteristically *transform* into birds at night.

This recitation of Yoruba gods and heroes is intended to be suggestive rather than exhaustive, for with many hundreds of gods, the case cannot easily be otherwise. Some few of these gods and heroes intrude the world of men as works of affecting presence, whether as a carved figure (e.g., Eshu), or as ritual device considered to be the necessary and sufficient circumstances for the presence of the god (e.g., a mound of earth for Eshu, staffs for the orishas Oko and Osanyin [plates 19, 20], a wand for Shango, and masks for Egungun and witches). In some instances, a god may be given in both figure and device (Eshu, for instance, in carving and in mound). In other cases—most notably Olorun, the creator god himself—neither is done. Thus among the Yoruba does the ancient mythologemic inheritance (St. John calls it *the Word*) incarnate into presence.

Mythologems are also *things that can communicate* (Ifa divination [plate 21], the brass figures of the Ogboni society [plate 22], the staff of Osanyin [plate 20]); *things that can punish* (the Ogboni rods, wrongly sworn); *things that can maintain* (the twin figures [plates 23–25] properly treated can maintain the well-being of the family); *things that can alter* (by essence: the Gelede mask [plates 5–8] *becomes infused with the power of good and evil*). But mostly, alterations concern people: witches become birds; in twins, one becomes two. (Recall the non-Yoruba belief that Yoruba people can convert children into money-spewing automatons.)

Mythologemic times abound in a society where individual lives are subject to complex, highly socialized, and successive (syndetic) role-taking. There are the times of *puberty*, the times of elevation in the group by *marriage*, the times of *title-taking*, the times of *gaining membership in the most elevated and secret of the various societies*—concerned with the well-being of the earth and of the people—and finally the *time of dying*. Like a weft moving back and forth across the liminal warps of time, the never-quiescent time of the ancestors slides: the eternal present, without possibility of either future or past.

Mythologems are analogic estates and processes of the consciousness, eidetic inheritances to all mankind, endowing him with both wholeness and depth of being. They inform both our waking and our sleeping hours, and their function in the work of affecting presence is critical. For in affecting presence they are present—in the urgency of their primal energies—as cognizers of us, their witnesses. That this is so is not the result of legerdemain. The power with which they disturb our sleep, the power in which they are healingly present in ritual, the depth to which they gratify us or move us in art—these are all the reward of the inalienable property of the mythologem. The mythologem is a deep power of the work, incarnating a basic consciousness-of in the work's facticity. It is the basal metabolism of the work's being.

4   THE POWERS OF
                THE MYTHOFORM I

One can identify the mythologemic by the symptoms: its broad dispersion among man's cultures; its obscure, primal, troubling import that raises to the order of *the important* every work it invests as motif, morphé, and theme. These markers guide us into areas of human experience we would not ordinarily have thought of as of the world of the mythopoetic. Thus, for example, in music the scale can be regarded as of mythopoetic import, as also can harmony and rhythm; and, in dance, the translation of the body's movements into symmetry (or asymmetry) and regularity are mythopoetic. But there are other fonts of consciousness' energy, and they too empower the work with urgency. These powers are of the cultural options made among the powers of the mythologemic and of the particular construction given them. These culture-specific configurations comprise the mythoform. I will now examine this font of the work's power, choosing to study the sculptures of the Yoruba. I opt not to work with all the arts, because, *mutatis mutandis,* what in any given culture is structurally and dynamically true in one art tends to be true in the others as well.

In a strongly homogeneous culture, dance and sculpture tend identically to enact the body in space, with the result that sculpture seems to become "frozen dance" (to extrapolate from Schelling's invention that architecture is "frozen music")[1] and vice versa. The sculptural and balletic mythologemic theme one first notes is that which respects the body's relationship to gravity, whether it is pulled toward it or is released from it. We encounter the former mythologemic condition in the sculpture and dance of

1. I am indebted to my colleague Professor Lillian Furst for the attribution of this lexical invention.

much of the world—among the tribal peoples of Oceania, North and South America, and Africa. The latter mythologem, release from gravity, is more rare: India's multiarmed Sivas, and our eloquent arabesques, indicate the nature of the rare phenomenon. But there are also respects in which dance and sculpture diverge mythologemically. The most notable example of this divergence is found in that singularly dramatic plastic mythologem—so broadly distributed among the "tribal" peoples of the world—of that dynamic of ratios which reveals itself in a greater-than-normal largeness of head, with respect to the rest of the body. Further, legs and arms may either be much shorter than is normal in the human body (save among dwarfs and infants), or else they may be much longer. If it is the case that large-headedness mythologemically appears, one can be quite certain that its opposite will also mythologemically be present as an option to human expressiveness. Thus one variously finds a contrary emphasis upon a head size markedly smaller than is ordinarily the case among actual human beings (plate 26 illustrates both small head and long limbs). Of course, it is equally mythologemic that there should exist in the repertory of the human consciousness a notion of the "wholly other," for the Almighty is perhaps frequently conceived of as different from rather than as similar to the corporeal predictabilities of the human frame and feature.

Quite clearly is it possible to distinguish the mythologemic in human behavior. Equally clearly is it possible to recognize the mythoformal, for if there were no universe of the mythoformal, differences among human cultures would not exist. The mythoform is a culturally specific system of processes chosen from among the mythologemically dynamic processes of the consciousness' execution of acts and things (syndesis, synthesis; intension, extension; continuity, discontinuity). The mythoform dictates the general character of the culture, and the culture's particular identity is to be seen as resulting from special formulations of these processes and, undoubtedly, other processes as yet unrecognized. The mythoform operates so as to shape into a consistent wholeness all that the people of a given culture are and do.

The mythoform is imperatival, defining and enforcing the conditions under which we perceive and embody our worlds, and screening out or reinterpreting those stimuli which fail to conform to our mythoformal grids. The mythoform is absolutely existential; it exists prior to concept about it, prior to distinctions of the self-world into space and time. It is of a sort whose true nature is unknown and perhaps even unknowable to the meager facilities of those languages with which we probe such preverbal depths.

Similarly, it is only by the grossest kind of license that I may speak of it as a "system." "System" is what it achieves but not what it *is*. It undoubtedly *is* not of parts, a condition the word "system" would suggest, but abides rather in a simple one-ness, the elemental consistency-dynamic which makes the world and our existence in it recognizable, predictable, and real.

I cannot say how it is that the mythoform invests and originates some of the contents, constructions, and usages of such cultural phenomena as social systems, economies, and languages. Yet without fail we can perceive it self-declaratively present in the work of affecting presence. In aesthetic space, time, and dynamic, the shapes and processes of the culture-specific urgencies are stated, restated, played with—the theme of the possibilities of our sentient existence and its variations. Such works enact the terms of our consciousness itself, both in that consciousness' own ways, im-mediatively, and for its own sake. Our works of affecting presence confirm the rightness of our consciousness of self and world by reifying the shapes and energies of that consciousness, confirming itself to itself. We who will search for these terms in a particular culture will find them creating into a systemic whole the diversities, often apparently irreconcilable, that a total corpus of works of affecting presence seems to present.

The fact that the nature and causes—and the systemicity—of presence may not be recognized as such by a people whose works might be the subjects of one's concern, or that such a people do not "know" the nature of their mythoform is even less a cause for our wonder than that they also do not "know" the restless generators or the phonemes of their language. As grammatical and sonal systems order the speech of even the most unlearned, causing them to speak and sing in system whether or not they *know* that system, so does the mythoform order and direct our consciousness, bringing behavioral order into our world.

The enactment of the mythoform is the "natural" construction of the self, others, the world, and the universe they share. Its processes empower believability into those works of affecting presence concerning which (among all man's works) we say that they *exist* . . . have being. We believe in works of affecting presence as we never do in mere objects, which though they may reflect the imperatives of the mythoform do not incarnate it, breathing it as the essential condition of their existence. The mythoform charges the work's space, time, and dynamic into the being of presence. The mythoformal constellation of consciousness informs every act of our being, as "genes" inform each cell of the various tissues of our bodies.

Although extension and intension, continuity and discontinuity, and syndesis and synthesis are primary terms of the mythoform, they are by no means sufficient to enable us to distinguish, let us say, amongst all intensive-continuous-syndetic cultures. That consistency which distinguishes the Yoruba from the Ibo, and the Ibo from the Papuan cultures—each of which is intensive, continuous, and syndetic—is to be sought in other dynamics. Even so we must not neglect to recognize that the three categories of energies with which we are here concerned are subject to varying degrees of strength and style of emphasis from culture to culture. And we must note that these variations will themselves produce profound cultural differences. We shall see something of the consequences of unequal emphasis upon one of them when we further consider the works of the Yoruba, below.

The study of the mythoform places the order of address of anthropological inquiry prior to that of ethnographic studies. Less than any other kind of anthropological investigation does it require the testimony of one native to the culture as "informant." Its assumption that the work of affecting presence is its own informant, saying more of itself than the indigene would probably know, makes it anthropologically unique. In such acts of consciousness, the steadfast and invariant presence of the mythoform will be clearly apprehended if one but use sufficient imagination to ascertain how it is that different enactments of a certain feature of the mythoform—intension, let us say—are in fact similetic equivalents one of the other, differing manifestations of the pulse of a common energy.

The cultural mythoform is to be seen as a special, hominid modification of those behavioral maps inborn in other animals. In man, however, except at the highest order of generalization (e.g., man is a "religious animal," a "speaking animal," "Homo ludens"), it is not the content of behavior which is determined by his kind—as the content of a bird's nesting behavior and flight imperatives are; it is rather the case that man inherits an imperative to harmonic configuration, to pattern. Man's is a structural program, not an inventory. The possibilities of substantive variability are reasonably great in his behavior. This creates such a degree and kind of behavioral variation from the people of one culture to those of the next that in any other animal such variations would define new species. Cultures, in this respect, are thus to be seen as *faux species*. It is clear that mythoformal differences are the agencies of this phenomenon.

The mythoform is not only the specifically human version of a primitive life-force common to all living forms, that in ascending order as one mounts the evolutionary scale permits greater complexity of behavior; it is also the interface between the nature of consciousness and the nature of that reification of consciousness into culture. The mythoform is the highest anthropological level we can reach. On this side of it lie the rich diversities of ethnographic particularities; on that side lies humanity itself.

Before proceeding, we had best pause to observe that ambiguous phenomena are to be found between the clearly mythologemic and the clearly mythoformal. Whether these tend chiefly toward the mythologemic or the mythoformal will be argued in accordance with the degree to which one prefers to concentrate upon either a genetic or a historical notion of the nature of the human consciousness. Thus, there are not only cultures, but there are complexes of cultures—regions wherein the constituent cultures tend to be more like one another in certain notable respects. We designate such regions to be "culture areas." Under the suasion of the notion that common features reveal common ways of being conscious and enacting consciousness of the world, we must conclude that in common plastic behaviors such cultures share some mythoformal condition of being. If the mythoform of the first order is cultural, that of the second order is areal. And so it goes, until one comes to that more diffuse point at which it can be maintained that in such and such highly general respects the sculpture all over Africa may be said to exhibit certain common processes and structures of enacting consciousness.[2] Indeed, even beyond these similarities there exist—in the sculptures of Oceania, of cultures of North and South America —certain plastic myths which suggest an ancient condition of enacting the plastic consciousness.

The wide and irregular distribution of these myths would argue that this condition is perhaps more ancient than that highly evolved one we encounter from the Upper Paleolithic.

On the basis of these considerations, therefore, it is clear that beyond the cultural, we face two further main streams of mythic: one, those trans-cultural plastic mythologems of broad distribution among Homo sapiens; and the other, restricted to wide African distribution. The features of this latter sort are striking as plastic inventions—distinctively peculiar to Africa —and one can only conclude from the fact they occur in such broad and dis-continuous dispersion that they own a primal Africanness.

The traits I shall consider of the first class are intension, big-headed-

2. Robert Plant Armstrong, *Forms and Processes of African Sculpture.*

ness, and deemphasis of the extremities; those of the second class are facial striations, neck/wrist rings, zig-zag legs, unitive shoulder-pectoral masses, and forward shoulder-arm masses.

The features of the first class:

Intension. I know of few traditional pieces of African sculpture which unambiguously enact extension. The arms of some Ashanti akwaba (plate 27) have what almost appear to be vestigial arms that extend straight out into horizontal space; but those arms are so small as to lead us to question whether this is indeed extension (it would seem that at minimum, to be called "extensive" a feature ought to exceed the line drawn downward from the widest measurement of the head). Further, there are pieces now and again which seem to show extension (see the Bassa female, plate 28). The most conspicuous act of extension I am aware of in African sculpture is in the Wanyamwesi figure (plate 26), where the arms extend dramatically into space. But energies toward extension are rare and seem almost always to be stopped short of fulfillment. The simple fact is that the preponderance of African sculptural figures seem to practice a near columnarity, with their arms straight or slightly curved, and hugged quite closely to the body (plate 29). When the figure is seated, its arms still intend, the hands holding a bowl or supporting a baby (plate 30).

Big-headedness. Relatively small heads do occur in African sculpture, most notably in iron pieces, though in wood as well, as we have seen. But largeness of head is a common theme, extending all the way from the extraordinary relative size of the head of the akwaba to the less excessive relative greatness of the head of a Yoruba ibeji (plates 23–25).

Deemphasis of the extremities. Whereas the greater-than-life size of the sculpted African head bespeaks the emphasis of an extremity, the hands and feet tend in general to be of modest size and are generally subject to summary sculptural treatment. Exceptions are to be noted among the Anyi, who although they tend not to exaggerate the relative size of the hand, sometimes give marked attention to the carving of a hand and fingers, with points of articulation lovingly shown (plate 9a). Further, the Yoruba tend sometimes to exaggerate the size both of hands and of feet, without, however, lavishing the same careful attention to structural detail. The Chokwe, in contrast, very often exaggerate the sizes of both hands and feet (plate 31).

Several features of the second class (the Pan-African motifs) are as follows:

Facial striations. One must accept the notion that the mere existence of these general plastic themes overrides any indigenous explanations to which various instances of them are subject. This is to say that whether the lines which cover the faces of sculptures be interpreted as scarifications (the Gelede mask, plate 5), or simply as design elements (Basongye Kifwebe masks, plate 32), or whether it be presumed that they result from technological process (as in the gold masks of the Baoule, plate 34), they are to be regarded as the same plastic motif, the same phenomenon of consciousness. Facial striations are ancient, being encountered also among the ancient Sao of Lake Chad. And the distribution of the motif is as broad as it is ancient. The Dan of Ivory Coast use it (plate 36), as do the Bacham of Cameroon (plate 33), and the Hongwe of Gabon (plate 35 and 35a).

Neck rings. Such differences of indigenous "explanations" of a plastic motif can also be found in other motifs. Thus neck rings are interpreted as rolls of fat (Mende, plate 37), and as layers of beads (Benin, plate 38). But whatever the particular verbal interpretation, all instances are to be regarded, sculpturally, as a manifestation of a common motif. They are also to be found among the Bassa, the Ebrie, and the Anyi of the Ivory Coast (plates 28, 40, 45), the people of the Bissagos Islands (plate 39), the Bangwa of Cameroon (plate 41), the Basongye, the Kuyu, and the Dengese of Zaire (plates 42, 43, 44).

Zig-zag legs. One of the most stunning of the African plastic motifs is the zig-zag, most commonly encountered in the execution of legs, although among the Lega the executions of the chest-abdominal-pelvic-leg masses are in rare instances reduced to zig-zags. Zig-zag legs exploit a diamond shape. This may be enacted once $\langle\rangle$, once and a half $\langle\langle$ times, or twice $\langle\langle$. This motif is also widespread among African peoples. Thus it is to be found among the Mumuye, the Turka, and the Afo of Nigeria (plates 46, 47, 49), the Kaka of Cameroon, the Lega, and the Boma of Zaire (plates 48, 50, 51).

The zig-zag motif is to be seen as dynamic. It results from a notion of the body as a related succession of masses: shoulders, chest and abdomen, pelvis, and legs, each of which is subject to separate balletic emphasis. Indeed, dance movement tends to be from the shoulders to or through the abdomen, and to or through pelvis and, successively, upper legs. As a matter of fact, this syndetic thrusting in dance seems to generate two further plastic motifs: (1) The definition of a shoulder-pectoral continuum—an ancient motif already present in the Sao terra cottas, and used today by peoples as distant one from the other as the Montol of Nigeria (plate 52) and the Senufo of the Ivory Coast (plate 53). (2) A variation upon this theme is the thrust *(thrusting)* shoulders seen, for example, among the Fang of Gabon (plate 54) and the Mbole of Zaire (plate 55), two examples I have chosen to indicate something of the outer perimeters of this motif's distributions.

Each of these plastic motifs is to be seen as a means to the achievement of syndetism, whether visually or kinetically. The reduction of legs to a series of vertically related triangles—no less than vertically successive neck or wrist rings, or than consecutive, concentric facial striations—is an instance of vertical homomorphous repetition.

The Yoruba participate in several of these general African sculptural motifs: facial striations (plates 6, 21); neck rings (in the ancient modeled and/or cast heads from the Yoruba city of Ife, the motif sometimes appears as rolls of fat); and zig-zag legs (Shango staff, plate 56). Yet the Yoruba mythoform is not to be found in the Yoruba sculptors' selection of generalized African plastic motifs. These speak to a larger order of African affecting reality. The mythoform of the Yoruba lies this side of those elements (the other "side" being the domain of the clearly mythologemic), and is to be defined, as among the terms identified in this book, as a special exploitation of intension, continuity, and syndesis.

The corpus of Yoruba sculpture, insofar as I am aware, holds no work as radically intensive as the Waja figure (plate 4). Nor does one find, at the other extreme, any marked interest in extension. Where the arms of figures are to be found at positions other than straight alongside the body or slightly akimbo—both of these traits characterizing ibeji figures, for instance—the general tendency is for them to be flexed at a 45- to 90-degree angle. It is overwhelmingly the case that under such circumstances the hands are carved holding objects (see the Epa mask, plates 57–59). In such cases, it is clear that the sculptor's interest lies not in extension for its own sake. One should also note that usually, though not exclusively, arms extend frontally into space. Where lateral extension is to be found (see the figures atop the Olowe bowl, plate 3), arms are interlocked, so that we once again see the Yoruba carver's determination to deemphasize spatial extension.

In order to dramatize the Yoruba interest in intension, I have selected a male figure associated with Shango, the divinity of thunder (plate 10). Examination of this piece, attending its elegant lines and subtle hankering toward inner-core, will, I believe, reveal more about the processes of intension than I can reveal through prose. At the same time, the reader is once again invited to study the bowl (plate 3), there to discover that on some occasions a preoccupation with a further dynamic—syndetism—will tend to give counter-statement to the simple power of intension. For even though all the figures enact intension, the total effect of the piece is rather more one of a unified dispersion than of the elegance so characteristic of many Yoruba works.

As for continuity, one finds that Yoruba continuity is often achieved atomistically, through the pervasion of points rather than through long lines. In music this pointillism is made manifest through repeated percussive events rather than through the use of long melodic lines. In design pointillism happens as well, especially in the works of some contemporary painters, where backgrounds may be executed as a dense repetition of identical floral designs, or encircled dots.[3] Pointillism also occurs in Yoruba cloth designs. Yet nowhere is it more pronounced than in the beadwork at which Yoruba craftsmen are so wonderfully adept (see plate 64). The fact that so powerful a work as a crown is executed in beads suggests something of the power immanent in the pointillistic technique. In this penchant toward pointillism, one sees that there exists a gradient between continuity and syndetism, such that the former may be called a special instance of the latter.

If not the most difficult of the mythoformal imperatives for us to grasp, syndesis at least seems on the surface to be the most unfamiliar, though we enact it in the "logic" of our dreams, in our compulsive, magical behaviors, and in the patterns of acquisition we establish—whether these be the saving of money or the collecting of art.

The human consciousness seems capable of but two kinds of culture-creation: that which is accumulative, and that which is eventuating or organic. In the latter case, c "grows out of" b, just as b in its turn eventuated from a. One may not say this of the syndetic, where linear, evolutionary growth tends less to dominate than does ardent proliferation. Syndetic growth, according to our Western view, may seem gratuitous, for we know

---

3. In the event a reader wishes to pursue this further, he may turn to my discussion of "Ogogoro Man" in *Wellspring,* listed in the bibliography below.

naught of the "logic" of its increase. We do not even know whether its causes are external or inherent. The syndetic is sequential; the synthetic is consequential. The syndetic enacts a conviction that additivity and supplementarity reign as the order of things; the synthetic exists within a world view that is contrastive and resolutional. The former is accretive; the latter is dialectical. The syndetic seems to create a wholeness which is the sum of its constituent wholenesses; the dialectical creates a wholeness that is sum-transcendent. Resolutionality implies the existence of the discontinuity of oppositions between the extremes it defines, whereas supplementarity assumes complements, or repetitions—not an ascent of ever-mounting highs, successively unlike one another, but a continuum of similitudes. Among the Yoruba, for instance, infancy and old age seem not antithetical, for the one appears to be continuous with the other through the interposition of processes of reincarnation.

In the case of the syndetic work of affecting presence, each act of supplementation is in itself a complete fullness, absolutely in possession of *all* or both that kind and degree of vital force appropriate to the integer added. I am here thinking of the syndetism of "tribal" peoples, and not of that fashionable sort (e.g., collage) employed by some of our contemporary artists. The "tribal" syndetism employs an arithmetic of wholes, which, contributory though they might be to the achievement of a further whole, cannot be *parts* (which by definition are denied wholeness). Thus a tree is a wholeness out of which—after proper recognition of its wholeness through libation and prayer—a mask is made. That mask is in its turn a wholeness; properly invoked it is entitive, a being. It may have a cock sacrificed to it, and that cock is a wholeness, as are both the man who wears it and the society in behalf of whom it is invoked. These wholenesses are related one to the other in a linear and accumulative fashion.

It is the constituents of the synthetic work which are parts. The pigment of which the European Romantic painting is made or the marble that hosts the statue, neither has any reality of its own that is of aesthetic independence—in contrast with the tree, which is a vital force to be reckoned with, of which the carving is made. Marble and pigment are but parts of subsequent, eventuating works. Supplementation and resolution, then, are the characteristic energies of the syndetic and the synthetic, respectively. These energies and the works into which they eventuate are the points of our most immediate concern.

The syndetic work is unconfined; it is a stone cast into the waters of time, the rings of its impact ever more broadly encompassing. No matter whether the item is temporal (music) or spatial (a carving), the syndetic work strives to become pure time. All syndetic works are temporal works. Nowhere has this movement been more dramatically obvious than among the Maya, for whom the spatial world seems to have been but a special dimension of the temporal one.

The syndetic work disperses energy; the synthetic work conserves it. And perhaps the movement of the synthetic work lies in the directions not of the realization of pure time but rather in the achievement of pure space. Our explicit Western preoccupation with "form" tends to assert our determination to endow time with the shapes of space, rather than the other way around.

The "wholeness" of the syndetic work is so different from that of the synthetic work that it is best to call the two conditions by different names. The fact that the syndetic work's growth is by sequentiation rather than by consequentiation tends to make it open-ended. It thus does not have a "beginning, a middle, and an end," each of which carefully entails—or is entailed by—the other. I have asked Yoruba dancers, whose movements are indefatigably repetitive, how they know when a dance is finished. They have responded that they ascertain this from the drums, but I have not found that the drummers recognize any necessary, developmental principle determining when they have achieved an entailed, organic wholeness and when they must therefore discontinue playing. This is a problem requiring field research. One must inquire of various peoples in what ways wholeness might be perceived to exist. I suspect that the termination of a dance or of a session of music, in syndetic cultures, comes about from external (social) conventions or (individual) preferences, or from such other external factors as fatigue or boredom.

Rather than of *wholeness,* one ought to think of syndetism in terms of *fullness.* Some works are modest in their requirements for supplementation (the twin figures of the Yoruba, for example, require a simple feeding of gruel or wine but once in five days), while the requirements of others are immodest, some especially powerful pieces requiring, formerly, the ultimate supplementation of the sacrifice of human life. Whatever their needs, the works must be enriched, each to its appropriate degree.

The power of the syndetic is the power of physical and metaphysical repletion. Some kinds of supplementation are generated by the various items constituting the work: the repeated patterns of the drums and the steps of the dancers, the enrichments of the costume and the mask. These are all "physical." But in other cases these are insufficient. Here the switch of sacrifice is thrown, and the requisite power is transferred from other sources, whether these be objects (beads, coins), foods, drinks, or lives. This is "metaphysical" supplementation.

As needs vary, so also do the degrees of the power which must be invoked. Thus it is difficult to give precise definition to an invoked work. One thing clear is that the work—because it is so often without any features we could in our understanding of the terms call "beginning," "middle," and "end"—seems tubular, a condition achieved in the columnar forms of so many syndetic sculptures and in the "tubes" of rhythmic repetitions in drumming and dancing. The work tends to suggest a fuse through which ignition flows. A section of high-tension wire has only arbitrary commencement and termination as well.

The syndetic work's power is in marked measure the power of time itself, not only the time in which it is enacted, but time-absolute—utter continuity of person, or of king and of state, of the particular people, and of mankind. In such measure, the individual man fails. So also do those pieces intended to cope with this sempiternal power we experience linearly as time. Thus as man is sometimes at the height of his personal powers and sometimes not, so is the piece; and as man weakens from all his powers and dies, so does the piece. A new person steps into the place of the old; even so, a new piece is made to take the place of the one that grew too feeble. The whole performance in which the piece is invoked, that is the work. The work remains. We may find this odd to understand, for we tend to think of the work after our own European model, where the sculpture or the dance or the musical piece is the work itself. The piece—the item—is transient in the aesthetic of invocation.

I shall observe in passing that the view here suggested is analogous to the views even of the human individual held in the syndetic and the synthetic cultures. In the syndetic culture, the individual is a point in a diachronic lineage, growing into and declining from that fullness proper to him. Indeed, among the Yoruba (via reincarnation) the soul in successive reappearances in different bodies constitutes a pattern, a rhythmic repetition, through eternity. This all stands in contrast to our own notion, according to which the individual stands in uniqueness at the end of a process which reaches back in his awareness no further than his parents or grandparents, and in his belief, most probably no further than himself. He is not so much but a point in a continuum, but a singular end product to whom antecedents and progeny are equally irrelevant. Just so are his works of art points in stellar solitudes.

We know that metaphysical syndetism—the accretion of essences—occurs variously in the world. It occurs not only among the so-called primitive peoples of Africa, Oceania, and the Americas, but also among those of medieval and Renaissance Europe. There it was to be found, for instance, in the gift-endowed, miracle-working statues of the Virgin, as well as in various other items of power in the Christian rites. Indeed, metaphysical— or essential—syndetism is perhaps more basic than physical syndetism. Further, it does not lend itself to the borrowing of a modernist aesthetic, as does physical syndetism in collage, assemblage, decoupage, where it exists in a wholly secular mode—the trappings without the force of the powers of which syndetism was originally enactive.

If we take the trouble to look, we shall clearly recognize that the Yoruba aesthetic is syndetic, an aesthetic of power. Thus, as I have observed, twin figures exist, and they are what they are not because of any visual or "formal" virtuosity of their execution we may recognize but rather because of the fact that they are vital—receiving baths, food, cosmetics, and other personal recognitions, and dispensing protection. Perceptible excellence is not at all causative of their aesthetic status; power is, and this power waxes and wanes according to the treatment the wooden entities are accorded.

Still, I cannot speak of the Yorubas' metaphysical supplementation, those increases in the power of a work which result from sacrifices made to it—whether these be of blood, of cowries, or of wealth—for we do not know enough. If anthropologists are ever to understand the nature of the aesthetic, they must address ranging inquiries into the nature, the transferability, and the orders and equivalences of power. Our only alternative, therefore, is to study those syndeses we are able to *observe* and to infer from observations.

I have said the most apparent of the mythologemic variables which make for the cultural distinctiveness of the mythoform from people to people is *relative emphasis*—whether greatest emphasis is placed upon syndesis/synthesis on the one hand, or upon either intension/extension or continuity/discontinuity on the other. Clearly the genius of the Yoruba is to be characterized above all by their great focus upon syndesis. Indeed, the Yoruba explore syndesis with such richness and diversity that one might think of their "philosophy" as one we would call "syndetism," enacted both as a principle of *knowing* and as the practice of enrichment of works. Let us first attend the phenomenon of epistemological syndetism.

I am not alone in observing the manifestations of this Yoruba predisposition. Thus Margaret and Henry Drewal write, "Whatever the deep symbolism of doubling, it is probable that it somehow renders *eka* [a particular drumming sequence] more powerful." And Marilyn Houlberg observes that for ibeji, "beans are cooked with oil. Oil is to pacify trouble and so are beans. Therefore oil and beans cure double trouble." Robert Farris Thompson notes the syndesis of essence when he writes, "The emergence of this special refinement of iron [a 'characteristic sheen'] is achieved by prolonged and carefully controlled heating in a fire with bellows creating magic charismatic strength."[4]

Such evidences suggest syndesis to be a pervasive, mythoformal urgency of Yoruba culture. I suspect, therefore, that the *item* of affecting presence, as well the *work* of which the item is a supplementation, exists as a cluster of points established among the numerous intersecting lines of several systems of syndetic enrichments to be found in affiliations of the work. These affiliations are not immediately apparent. Further, I suspect that these systems are not without order. Thus I shall attempt to show as much for two kinds of Yoruba works.

It is characteristic of the work of virtuosity that it abides in discreteness. This is the natural result of an aesthetic dedicated to the autonomy of the perceptible item, where it is the internal energies of the piece that are generated and attended. This stands in contrast to the work of invocation, in which energy syndetically derives from host sources external to the work as such. In the aesthetic of invocation, the work exists at the point of maximal intersection of all those energy flows which establish the work's complicated power nexus.

Our aesthetic ethnocentrism requires not only that we see the Yoruba work of affecting presence in a context of virtuosity and—perhaps—beauty, but also that we see the work as a thing unto itself—both in the fact that

---

4. Margaret and Henry Drewal, "Gelede Dance of the Western Yoruba," p. 41; Marilyn Houlberg, "Ibeji Images of the Yoruba," p. 25; Robert Farris Thompson, *Black Gods and Kings: Yoruba Art at UCLA,* p. 10/3.

we tend to confound the item with the work, and in the fact that we tend to see the various cults and their works as discrete. But in fact, a given piece of a certain cult exists at the intersection of numerous streams of force from which it draws power. A piece—a work, indeed—is thus more nearly appropriately seen as a culturally defined particularity of a most complex affiliation of divers powers.

In order to reveal some portion of this complex of powers, we shall consider ibeji figures and Gelede masks, two categories of pieces that seem to be very similar with respect to the structures of their reaching into the power fountains of their culture. Both of these works characteristically occur as pairs, although one does encounter single twin figures. In both cases, one finds pairs either of the same or different sexes. In fact, the Gelede dance uses both mixed and identical pairs, for Efe, the chief mask whose dancing opens the ceremony, is paired with his wife who precedes him in the festival; subsequently, paired female masks are danced, as are paired Gelede buffalo masks.

The doubling noted by Houlberg and the Drewals we find elsewhere among Yoruba works—in Janus-faced figures, for example. And the Shango stone celt is invariably doubled in the sculpture of the Shango's top (plates 11, 12, 13). Indeed, doubling defines the necessary and sufficient condition for the Shango staff to exist, its sculptural details otherwise revealing nearly total diversity. In fact, there is one Shango staff in which *doubling* is doubled —a face upon each of the outward edges of the paired celts (plate 14). Edan Ogboni (plate 22), the chain-linked brass figures of the earth cult which are of signal importance in the ritual life of the cult, are also paired, identical male and female figures; even as though they were themselves twins, though I am aware of no clear evidence that the making of twins is intended. In fact, there are striking relationships between ibeji and Shango on the one hand and Gelede and Ogboni on the other. The first relationship is commonly asserted in the literature. Robert Farris Thompson states that the son of Shango had nine sets of twins in nine places.[5]

A relationship exists between ibeji and Gelede as well. Thompson says that they work witchcraft,[6] and Henry Drewal reports Gelede dancers wearing breasts in the form of ibeji, or breasts upon which ibeji have been

5. Robert Farris Thompson, "Sons of Thunder: Twin Images among the Oyo and Other Yoruba Groups," *vide* p. 11.
6. Ibid.

carved or to which they are attached.[7] The Drewals also write, "When asked, 'Why do you dance two by two with the same masks?' Aribo responded, 'it is because women give birth to twins. . . . That's why there are two masks.' "[8]

Both twins and Gelede are thrice related to doubles: ibeji by virtue of their own doubleness, through their relationship to Shango, and through their connections with Gelede; and Gelede, too, by their own doubleness, by their affiliation with the Ogboni who punish witches, and through ibeji. Indeed, the relationships between twins and Gelede we may see as an all-important bridge binding two complex, different, and complementary (syndetic) systems.

But Gelede and ibeji are at the same time also rated in singularity—for the soul of twins is one not two; and the Gelede relate to Yemoja, goddess of rivers and of witchcraft (this would seem to be Gelede's negative aspect, causing infertility or death), and to Onile, goddess of earth in positive aspect (fertility and life). It is important to note that Yemoja and Onile (Iyanla) are *alternative singles,* and are not to be thought of as constituting a pair.

But by the patterns of their relationships, ibeji and Gelede do seem to constitute a pair, and we may say, therefore, that they stand fixed between the point of a system of pairings on the one hand and a system of singularities on the other, partaking of behaviors associated with both. The wickedness and self-indulgence of twins, the evil fearsomeness of witches (or the blessings of Onile and her gift of fertility)—these relate to one-ness. To pairedness one ascribes the twins' well-known charm as well as the blessings they bring; and to doubling one attributes the positive virtues of the mothers (their relationship to Shango, to Ifa, and to the number 16). If we may so dualize the Yoruba world, evenness appears to be positive, whereas oddness is negative, harmful, or magical. (But the two are to be seen as syndetically complementary rather than as oppositional.) Twins and Gelede are thus centered in ambiguity, for ambiguity is syndetic, it is complementary—two things or estates coexisting with the result that a reduction of single clarity results. Works are thus caught between positive and negative, and between certitudes (Ifa) and incertitudes (Eshu).

At this point we may identify other "even" and "odd" data which are connected with ibeji and Gelede:

7. Henry Drewal, "Gelede Masquerade: Imagery and Motif," p. 10.
8. Margaret and Henry Drewal, "Gelede Dance," p. 41.

EVENS

Four. There are four units in each half of the divining beads one throws for Ifa; Yemoja has four eyes.

Eight. Eight beads constitute the whole chain of divining beads.

Sixteen. There are sixteen orders (odu) of divination; and sixteen witches on the radial surface of the staff for the god of medicine, Osanyin (plate 20).

Two hundred fifty-six. This is the square of sixteen, and it is the number of categories constituting the sixteen odu (orders) of Ifa.

ODDS

Three. The symbolic indicator of Eshu, the god of indeterminacy; e.g., three stripes occur on calabashes made for him. (Further, figures for Eshu are sometimes paired, and Pemberton associates Eshu with Shango—thus further complicating his role as master of ambiguity.)[9] A further indication of Eshu's primary affiliation with oddness is to be found in the fact that dance for him, Thompson somewhere observes, is characterized by asymmetry.

Five. On the fifth day, ibejis are fed.

Nine. The number of twins born to the son of Shango.

Eshu is the trickster, the god of the world of circumstance and accident. He is the other half of the Ifa, that god who, because he alone knows the will of Olorun, the Creator Sky-God, presides over divination, reveals certainties. Eshu's face presides over Ifa's divining board, and libation is offered to Eshu before the divining is begun.

Ifa and Eshu define the realm of ambiguity by drawing its boundaries, and it is in ambiguity that ibeji and Gelede are located. Eshu affiliates with the earth (he is the god of crossroads); but Ifa, knowing the will of Olorun, is connected with the sky. The *pair* of them, then, syndetically complement one another; each is a function of the other. Thus, as uncertainty is great, certitude is small; and contrariwise, as certitude grows, uncertainty diminishes. The pairedness of the two of them balances the pairedness of ibeji and Gelede.

Eshu, we have seen, relates to the essence of one-ness. But Ifa relates to two-ness: there are two halves to the divining chain, and two design halves comprise the border of the divining board (plate 68b). Further, em-

9. John Pemberton, "Eshu Elegba: The Yoruba Trickster God," p. 22.

blems of Shango (Oshe Shango) sometimes appear carved on the borders of divining boards, further asserting two-ness in his essence.

If odds tend to be magical or evil, and evens positive and desirable, Eshu as the principle of one-ness can be—and in life is—predicated upon any even-ness, changing it into an odd-ness. (Thus, perhaps, the iconic significance of three—two plus one—which is his sign.) Thus is his image so common, so often found on the altars of other gods.[10] Reduce Eshu (subtract one from any uneven-ness), and even-ness reasserts. The relationships between these two gods circumscribe the fearful ambiguities to which all mortals are heir.

Earth is singular, as is sky, and ibeji and Gelede affiliate in both directions: ibeji and Gelede with the sky via monkeys and birds, and both with earth via their fertility functions; ibeji by occasioning blessings, Gelede by bringing about fertility.

I have diagrammed these and several other relationships, and the reader is referred to Figure 1 in order to perceive at a glance the complexly syndetic nexus at whose midpoints the work of affecting presence stands.

These connections are perhaps *not specifically known as such* by the Yoruba. In regard to the works, they do not constitute explicit points of doctrine in Yoruba belief. Yet they are behaviorally certain—they define networks in the Yoruba consciousness which are rather like spiders' webs: touch one at one point and all the subtle reticulation is set into response.

I doubt that there is any structure present in these networks that one might characterize as oppositional and resolutional. The Gelede-ibeji network, the odd-even network, the double-single network, and (if we follow through from Thompson's observation about dance) the "symmetrical-assymmetrical" network—all these exist in syndetic complementarity. There are doubtless patterns to be found among them, for whether syndetic or synthetic, human action is patterned. But such patterns tend to exist in supportive relationships—doubles upon doubles, or singles upon them, odds upon evens, etc.—rather than in resolutionally dialectical ones.

With the reaches of Yoruba syndetism so profound and pervasive, there is little room for wonder that Thompson, the Drewals, and Houlberg ascertain the repetitive atomisms in, or connected with, works of affecting presence. Where the dynamics of the method and style of a people's *being*

10. Ibid.

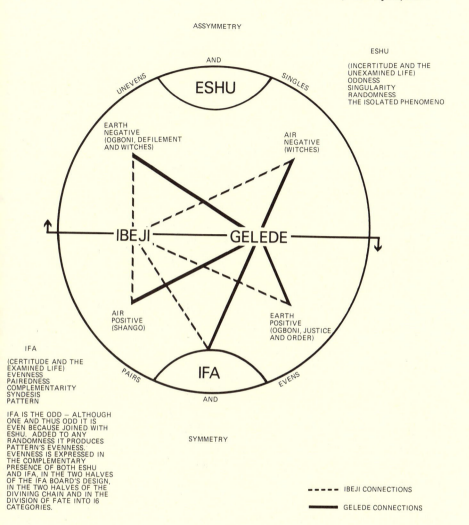

ASSYMMETRY

AND

SINGLES

UNEVENS

ESHU

ESHU

(INCERTITUDE AND THE UNEXAMINED LIFE)
ODDNESS
SINGULARITY
RANDOMNESS
THE ISOLATED PHENOMENO

EARTH
NEGATIVE
(OGBONI, DEFILEMENT
AND WITCHES)

AIR
NEGATIVE
(WITCHES)

IBEJI — GELEDE

AIR
POSITIVE
(SHANGO)

EARTH
POSITIVE
(OGBONI, JUSTICE
AND ORDER)

IFA

(CERTITUDE AND THE
EXAMINED LIFE)
EVENNESS
PAIREDNESS
COMPLEMENTARITY
SYNDESIS
PATTERN

PAIRS

IFA

EVENS

AND

IFA IS THE ODD — ALTHOUGH
ONE AND THUS ODD IT IS
EVEN BECAUSE JOINED WITH
ESHU. ADDED TO ANY
RANDOMNESS IT PRODUCES
PATTERN'S EVENNESS.
EVENNESS IS EXPRESSED IN
THE COMPLEMENTARY
PRESENCE OF BOTH ESHU
AND IFA, IN THE TWO HALVES
OF THE IFA BOARD'S DESIGN,
IN THE TWO HALVES OF THE
DIVINING CHAIN AND IN THE
DIVISION OF FATE INTO I6
CATEGORIES.

SYMMETRY

- - - - - IBEJI CONNECTIONS

GELEDE CONNECTIONS

SYNDETIC AMBIGUITIES OF IBEJI AND GELEDE

Figure 1.

conscious become self-reflexive substance—as is the case in the work of affecting presence—there we may expect we shall encounter the mythoform not once, and not in doctrinaire guise, but multitudinously; and we are brought face to face with it not only as fact but as celebration.

Ibeji and Gelede, we see, do not exist as explicit and conscientious synthetic eventuations of all these factors of their powers. Instead these connected factors are "resonances"—enrichments which exist in complex and patterned syndeses. Yoruba syndetism does indeed reach deeply and universally into the dynamic of Yoruba being, constituting their consciousness.[11]

Yet this network syndesis exists supplementarily with the further syndesis of both metaphysical (essences—blood, food, drink, medicine) and physical enrichments (e.g., clothing, cosmetics). It is to the latter of these that I now direct the reader's attention. In order to do this, I shall address this energy as it is to be encountered in the Yoruba carvings themselves, viewed in the whole of their corpus. We adopt this dedication to the largest view of the sculptural works because the level of our concern is anthropological, and it is anthropological because we are committed to seeing consciousness' enactment of certain behaviors which obtain as of the cultural order.

One of the simplest kinds of physical syndesis would seem to be the application of colors to the surface of a work, whether this means painting a mask in various colors (as the Yoruba polychrome their Gelede masks, their stools, and some of their shrine figures) or staining a work so as to cause its surface to be of one color throughout (see the Fang, plate 61). Color is applied sometimes for its visual delights, sometimes for its "medical" properties, and sometimes (doubly syndetically) for both—though it sometimes may be difficult to tell which kind of power a color might have. In the polychroming of their sculptures the Yoruba once again treat them as they treat themselves, for at certain times in their lives, Yoruba have white kaolin applied to their persons, or brick-red camwood powdered upon them. Blue is enormously important, being widely used in the polychroming of sculptures. Indeed, blue is the pervasive color of the Yoruba. A market throng is likely to be comprised nearly wholly of people—women chiefly—all or most of whom are wrapped in blue cloths and surmounted by lavish, blue headties. One should note (to employ the analytical terms here presented) that Fang monochromy is homomorphous, whereas Yoruba polychromy is heteromorphous.

---

11. I have already written on syndetism in traditional and contemporary design (*Wellspring,* pp. 73 ff.), and in narrative (*Wellspring,* pp. 61 ff., and "Tragedy—Greek and Yoruba: A Cross-Cultural Perspective").

As I have said, whether these applications are "merely" cosmetic or whether they are of medicinal value—and thus whether they are of the order of physical or of metaphysical import—I cannot clearly ascertain. I suspect, inasmuch as the Yoruba (not uniquely) are not averse to holding apparently contrary opinions regarding the same phenomenon at the same time, that both may be true simultaneously. To hold both views at once would be unsurprising in a syndetic culture. Thus it is a further characteristic of a syndetic culture that it should permit the imperative of accretion to override the Western-espoused "law" of noncontradiction. If a Yoruba is a Christian, he may very well also perform the practices of Islam, as well as some of those of the traditional animism/ancestorism. Power is desirable, wherever one might find it. Selection is not proscribed by sectarian niceties; access to power need not be foolishly circumscribed by mere theological discriminations. A carver I know accepts Islam; nonetheless it is without any sense of contradiction that he carves figures, or that these figures are as readily Christian as traditional.

However, is one only to observe of the various sculptural groups that one encounters—in quantity among the Yoruba—that their surfaces are treated either homomorphously or heteromorphously? Is it not further true that, in the case of groups of figures, those arrays are comprised either of the same or of different sorts of constituent figures, and these are either of the same or of different sizes? It is clear, insofar as such arrays are of the essence of Yoruba physical syndetism, that we must extend our terms so as to apply to them as well. Thus we may say, concerning items constituting an array of the same size and posture, that they are formally homomorphic, whereas those that show variations of size and posture are formally heteromorphous. And we shall say of those figures that are "the same" (all males, all females, all animals) that they are substantively homomorphous, whereas those which reveal differences (some human, some animal, some male, some female) are substantively heteromorphous.

Further, these arrays may be such that the constitutive figures are vertically arrayed (atop one another), laterally arrayed (with figures abreast of one another), ventrally arrayed (figures before and behind one another), and radially arrayed (figures in a circle). It is also possible for these arrays to co-occur in various combinations, although lateral and ventral array seem most frequently to be found together (see table 1).

This model makes it possible to say of the wood sculpture of the Baoule (for instance) that in general it does not exist in syndetic array—the

Table 1

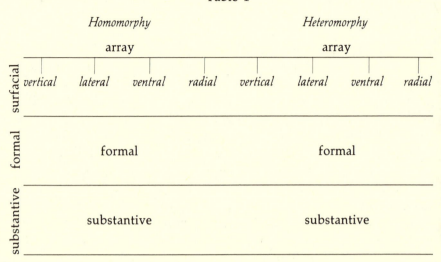

	Homomorphy array				*Heteromorphy* array			
surfacial	*vertical*	*lateral*	*ventral*	*radial*	*vertical*	*lateral*	*ventral*	*radial*
formal		formal				formal		
substantive		substantive				substantive		

exception being the occasional maternity figure (plate 74) which is formally, substantively (in that one is an adult and the other a babe), and ventrally heteromorphous—but that it is surfacially homomorphous. The Yoruba, on the other hand, present a very different case. Yoruba works in wood exist in vast numbers both singly and in sculptural array. These arrays can become very complex indeed (plate 59). However, because the only physical syndesis possible in the single work is that of surface, I shall here be concerned only with those marvelous arrays so characteristic of Yoruba wood sculpture.

I am not aware that surfacial homomorphy occurs in Yoruba sculpture. One sees carved doors *without* any color, but even though they are thus "monochromatic," one can hardly call this condition *syndetic.* On the contrary, Yoruba works which enjoy surfacial syndesis, whether single works or works of array, do so in heteromorphy—the application of colors, beads, cloth. But rather than continue the use of prose to illustrate these various types, I shall instead present in paradigmatic order a series of syndetic types, showing, wherever possible, Yoruba examples thereof.

1. surfacial homomorphy   figures same color throughout (plate 62)
2. surfacial heteromorphy   figures of different colors (plate 63)

3. formal vertical homomorphy	figures above and below of same size and disposition, of either or of both sexes (plate 64)
4. formal lateral homomorphy	figures side-by-side of the same size and disposition (plate 13)
5. formal ventral homomorphy	figures of same size, fore and aft, one after the other (plate 65)
6. formal radial homomorphy	figures of like size and disposition surrounding a piece, e.g., birds around a crown, or figures around the layers of a stool (plate 73)
7. formal vertical heteromorphy	figures of different sizes and/or dispositions, one atop the other, e.g., a housepost (plate 66)
8. formal lateral hetermorphy	figures of different dispositions (hereafter abbreviated "of different dispositions") standing abreast (plate 63)
9. formal ventral heteromorphy	figures of different dispositions, fore and aft of one another (plate 67)
10. formal radial heteromorphy	figures of different dispositions radially arrayed (plate 68)
11. substantive vertical homomorphy	figures of same sort (sex, species, social status, and irrespective of size or disposition) atop one another (plate 69)
12. substantive lateral homomorphy	figures of same sort in a row (plate 13)
13. substantive ventral homomorphy	figures of same sort front-to-back, as warriors in procession (plate 70)
14. substantive radial homomorphy	figures of same sort in circle, like four females atop lid of Olowe's bowl (plate 3)
15. substantive vertical heteromorphy	figures of different sorts atop one another (plate 71)

16. substantive lateral heteromorphy	figures of different sorts abreast— as the Epa, with large central figure, small woman on one side (that much is isomorphy) and rooster on other side—the touch that makes it heteromorphous (plate 57)
17. substantive ventral heteromorphy	figures of different sorts front-to-back (plate 72)
18. substantive radial heteromorphy	figures of different sorts in circle (plate 59)

One may say that Yoruba works are of two classes. First, there is the class comprised of pieces caused to be what they are by virtue of their investment with power through metaphysical, physical, and epistemological syndeses (i.e., sacrifices, prayers, dances, affiliations, etc. [metaphysical]; cosmetics and costumes [physical]; and—for instance—twinning [epistemological]). Second, there are those items that do not (or do not *clearly*) so host power, and which therefore tend not to be enriched with metaphysical syndeses, but which are rather characterized only by epistemological and physical syndeses. These latter works include houseposts, doors, offertory bowls, containers of various sorts, stools, and some shrine figures. These are pieces *in attendance.*

Although some of the works of the first group exist in pairs (Ogboni edan rods, ibeji), they tend not to exist in the ecstatic array we have observed in the Epa mask; the iron pieces for the god Osanyin (plate 20), where a dominant bird is surrounded by sixteen small birds, is a notable exception. The pieces which exist in array tend to be in attendance rather than in invocation, which is to say that such attendant pieces *serve* men and gods. They are useful pieces and/or decorative ones. It thus seems as though we see among the Yoruba the existence of two aesthetics: one of the power of invocation and one of the power of virtuosity. That virtuosity is not one that many of us in Europe and America might necessarily readily appreciate (indeed even among collectors of African sculpture, Yoruba pieces have until recently not been the greatest favorites), for it tends to be a virtuosity of syndesis. We, in contrast, more overwhelmingly tend to prefer virtuosity of synthesis: we opt for definitive resolutions; we seek extrication from a work, whereas the Yoruba (especially in the sacred works) seek intricate involvement.

It may be fair to say that the Yoruba more fully and more richly exploit the ranges of syndesis than most—and perhaps all—of the other peoples of Africa. One of the most notable exceptions are the Fon (Republic of Benin), whose complex brass compositions (plate 75) qualify their creators for inclusion among those who delight in the virtuosity of physical syndesis. But not even among the Fon—who, incidentally, are connected with Yoruba—does richness of syndetic invention achieve the exuberance of either degree or range that it does among the Yoruba. That which some observers have dismissed with the invidious designation "Yoruba baroque" is thus to be seen not merely as a kind of inconsequential excess, but rather as the essential working-out in sculpture of an aesthetic or extraordinary complexity.

In the aesthetic of invocation, the work as orchestration of all its invocable items exists in affecting presence not in space but in time. Thus even spatial works—masks and figures—are to be seen as empowered by their history and by the rites of their invocation of which they are part. In a work of invocation, we have seen, that piece (e.g., the mask) which in Europe and America we call "the work" is elsewhere but an item in the work, owning its identity, to be sure, but in itself lacking the metaphysical conditions of presence, which is to say being devoid of aesthetic significance. By and large, presence is—in most of Africa—a function of invocation. But in Yoruba works of array—attendant pieces—where there is no invocation, the aesthetic changes. Here the piece is not *item* but is, rather, *work*, just as in our own European aesthetic; and here delight derives from virtuosity. When the shift is from an aesthetic of invocation to one of virtuosity, the work of sculpture, even though it exists syndetically, is released from its reality in time and delivered over into a meaningful spatial existence. Yoruba attendant works, therefore, achieve virtuosity in exuberant spatial syndetism.

Is it thus the case that in this respect we should say that two aesthetics exist among the Yoruba? Certainly this would not be impossible, for in complex cultures where various publics are to be discerned, different aesthetics do simultaneously coexist. In the United States today we have various aesthetics—e.g., "classical" and "popular" (country, western, rock; comic-strip, pop, sentimental and realistic "calendar" visual art). As the two Yoruba aesthetics we have discerned are bound by a common preoccupation with syndetism, so do those various aesthetics of the United States share a consuming passion for the virtuosity of novelty.

Still, I do not think that one should conclude the existence among the

Yoruba of two aesthetics, one alternative to the other. It seems rather that the aesthetics of works of power and of works of attendance stand together in complementarity. There are not two Yoruba publics in this respect, but one; and the aesthetic of invocation is syndetically enriched by the addition of the aesthetic of virtuosity. Pieces of virtuosity stand next to pieces of invocation on altars and are carried in processions aimed at invocation. Syndetic attendance is their function.

One sees this Janus-aesthetic not only in the co-occurrence of works of both sorts, but even within the same work. Consider the Gelede mask (plates 5–8): it is *the mask itself* which exists within the aesthetic of invocation. This we know from the fact that masks can be found which are without any attendant elaboration. The Gelede as such exists simply by virtue of the conformation of the mask's face and shape to certain traditional requirements. These are requisite to the condition of being Gelede—and of the possibility of the mask's invocation through sacrifice, dancing, and the drumming addressed to Gelede (essential or metaphysical syndetism). But it is also the case that sculptures of attendance often adorn the top of the Gelede, works which are not causative of the "Geledeness" of the mask but which nonetheless supplement the work so that it is somehow "finer" (physical syndetism), and more powerful (metaphysical syndetism). I suspect that much the same kind of case obtains with respect to the Epa mask (plates 57–59), where the Janus-faced helmet mask is the invariable element in the mask, but where the surmounting sculptures often attain to great— and greatly variable—enrichments of spatial complexities.

We observe this same conjuncture of the aesthetics of essential and physical syndetism in the instance of the palace (afin) of a Yoruba king (oba). The traditional afin of a Yoruba city-state is an array of courtyards in nearly every case surrounded by chambers and apartments. These are set aside for servants, wives (some compounds for those of the present oba, others for the widows of the former oba), princes and princesses, and the oba himself. These courtyards are dedicated to various functions: audiences with townspeople, audiences with important strangers, recreation, privacy. Some are dedicated to the worship of special gods, as at Afin Oyo (figure 2) where there is a courtyard dedicated to the god Shango, an early king of that city. To say that because each "compound" is comprised of a courtyard and surrounding chambers that altogether they constitute a homorphous syndetic whole, is akin to saying that array is homomorphous merely because a piece is comprised of figures. As one counts on finer distinctions of composition to classify a sculptural array, so must one do so in architectural

arrays. Thus the marked diversity of *functions* allotted to the various compounds argues the afin to be substantively heteromorphous, just as their
diversity of size and composition asserts the absence of formal homomorphy. Yet the courtyard-chambers motif, so often repeated in the afin's
execution, suggests formal homomorphy. Clearly the subsantive heteromorphy and the formal homomorphy are radially arrayed.

The fact that we are here viewing the spaces of the afin as lived

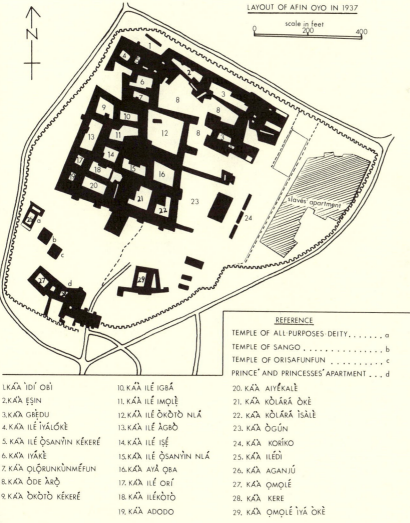

LAYOUT OF AFIN OYO IN 1937

scale in feet

REFERENCE

TEMPLE OF ALL·PURPOSES·DEITY . . . . a

TEMPLE OF SANGO . . . . b

TEMPLE OF ORISAFUNFUN c

PRINCE' AND PRINCESSES' APARTMENT . . . d

1.KÁÀ 'IDÍ OBÌ

2.KÁÀ ẸSIN

3.KÁÀ GBẸDU

4. KÁÀ ILÉ ÌYÁLÓKÈ

5. KÁÀ ILÉ ỌSANYIN KÉKERÉ

6. KÁÀ IYÁKÈ

7. KÁÀ ỌLỌRUNKÙNMÉFUN

8.KÁÀ ÒDE ÀRỌ

9. KÁÀ ÒKÒTÒ KÉKERÉ

10. KÁÀ ILÉ IGBÁ

11. KÁÀ ILÉ IMỌLẸ

12. KÁÀ ILÉ ÒKÒTÒ NLÁ

13. KÁÀ ILÉ ÀGBÒ

14. KÁÀ ILÉ IṢẸ

15. KÁÀ ILÉ ỌSANYIN NLÁ

16. KÁÀ AYÁ ỌBA

17. KÁÀ ILÉ ORÍ

18. KÁÀ ILÉKÒTÒ

19. KÁÀ ADODO

20. KÁÀ AIYÉKALÈ

21. KÁÀ KÒLÁRÁ ÒKÈ

22. KÁÀ KÒLÁRÁ ÌSÀLÈ

23. KÁÀ ÒGÚN

24. KÁÀ KORÍKO

25. KÁÀ ILÉDÌ

26. KÁÀ AGANJÚ

27. KÁÀ ỌMỌLÉ

28. KÁÀ KERE

29. KÁÀ ỌMỌLÉ ÌYÁ ÒKÈ

Figure 2.

spaces, as chambers and courts of enactments, prevents one from concluding, as he might do if he were to observe solely the ground-plan, that the afin's spatial enactments are in some sense "pure," that they are "abstract" syndetism. The notion of space for its own sake, such as one might encounter it in a Japanese rock garden, is—I believe—not to be found in Yorubaland.

There are further physical syndeses of the afin: the verandahs, which are numerous in the structure, tend characteristically to be supported by carved posts that themselves often exist in rich array; and the doors are often richly carved as well. Physical syndetism abounds, making of the afin the ultimate syndetic achievement of its culture—a work of physically syndetic virtuosity.

Yet the afin is more than this simply. Like the Gelede mask, it also exists simultaneously within the aesthetic of invocation. The afin is informed by the presence of the oba, it contains a courtyard dedicated to the worship of his head, and it hosts in its enclosures sacred altars to important gods. Rites critical to the well-being of the whole people are enacted within the courtyards and chambers of the afin. The afin exists at the heart of the city. And like the heart of the body, the afin pumps power, governance, and welfare throughout all the roads that radiate from it into the multitudes of compounds that constitute the city itself.

But if in the afin and the Gelede, the two aesthetics work together to create a greater syndetism within the aesthetic system itself, and to create a more dramatic sense of invocation, the marvelous offertory bowl carved by the Yoruba master, Olowe, from the city of Ise, seems to display naught but the excitement of syndetic virtuosity. Standing twenty-five inches, this piece enacts not only aesthetic virtuosities of complexity and execution that delight those of us heir to a Western European aesthetic of virtuosity, in our own aesthetic terms, but it also, and richly, enacts that virtuosity of physical syndetism which is as well known to the Yoruba as it is alien to us.

The work is a most enthusiastic array, a power of Yoruba visual form (plate 3). Homomorphously, it enacts, on its lid, a radial syndetism at once both formal and substantive. The ventral array of dominant figure with baby behind and with bowl before is both formally and substantively heteromorphous, just as are the members of that group of supporting figures below. With so much of the possible syndetic range exploited in one work, the piece must, one suspects, be characterized by a degree of syndetic virtuosity without many peers in the corpus of Yoruba works. One can only obscurely suppose the aesthetic richness and power (the power of enacting the mythoform) with which it endows any occasion, religious or social, to which it syndetically added its powers of virtuosity.

At least some music is to the temporal domain what the complexity of the physical syndetism of afin and Olowe bowl are to the spatial, realizing, it almost seems, absolute time by virtue of ever striving to achieve among several voices the densest possible pervasion thereof. I am thinking in particular of those musical activities where each drum of several separately, yet which utter complementarity (as is the case in the execution of the syndetic) searches out and relentlessly pursues an aspect of duration—duration through endless repetition of its own time-act. The interplay among these drums is an intricately syndetic realization of time. One can say of the Yoruba sculptural arrays that they have "content," which is to acknowledge that there is about them an identifiability—a concordance with things of the world—which can be communicated in words. But what are we to say is the "content" of the several drums' voices each insisting its own temporal essence? Where "melody"—which is to be seen as the "content" of music—is absent, whether in Yoruba drumming or in the most daring of contemporary Western music, there music seems to be "pure." We may say of such drumming that the maintained sound of each drum is both substantively and formally homomorphous and (by simile) ventral, whereas we may say of the synchronic instant—the cross-section of any musical instant—that it is "laterally" heteromorphous, both substantively and formally. Indeed, because there is no sense of melodic content (no "tune") to such music, one must maintain it inconceivable that there should be any disjuncture between form and substance. The notion of such disjunction is possible only with respect to a "pictorial" art, whether in line, color, volume, tone, or word.

In general, Yoruba sculptural works of array exist in frontality. This is to say that the visual address of the comprising figures is straight ahead —eyes, nipples, and knees all share common address and together create a syndetism of such points. There are exceptions, to be sure, most notably in a babe astride a mother's back, who most often (and quite reasonably) looks to the side (plate 30). Further, such frontal carvings, in the round and in array, tend to exist not with respect to one another, as would be the case in a European or American work, but rather with respect to the witness who perceives them face-on. It is as though syndetism would be sacrificed to synthesis were the figures to exist in interaction. In relief carving, one encounters greater complexity in this respect. On carved doors, figures sometimes exist both in profile and in full face, and also in visual address one to the other. Further, such relief figures carved frontally in body may exhibit face in profile, and those carved with body in profile may have face in full frontality. If one were to argue that the more complex the syndesis, the greater the existence of the work within the aesthetic of virtuosity, then surely the relief work would stand high in this aesthetic, alongside in-the-round pieces of the order of the Olowe bowl. A final observation: one does not find significant exploitation of mixed profiles (body frontal face in profile, or vice versa) where the two aspects bear to one another either more or less than 90-degree relationship, a fact which seems further to argue the primacy of frontality (lateral and ventral) in Yoruba sculptural address.

With respect to works of array, one may observe that there is no greater sense of the syndetic necessity of the inclusion of any given figure —no more sense of its eventuating ought-ness—than there is in a musical pattern of two-against-three of any subsequent repetition of that same beat. But quantity *does* rule in syndetism, and some pattern must prevail if chaos is to be defeated. And so the composition that in synthetic works derives from entailments of interrelationships (eye contact, tonal resolutions, etc.), in syndetism derives from the inevitably quantitative concern of *balance.* Where there exist such arrays of figures, a strong sense of balance obtains: a large figure will be flanked by smaller surrounding ones, and a sense of pattern will prevail. A study of such patterns of the achievement of balance would, in fact, provide a most rewarding insight into the Yoruba aesthetic.

Frontality plus the rhetoric of balance lend a sense of singularity to each of the comprising items of a Yoruba array. If a figure were to be removed, no psychological composition would be destroyed, as it would in a sculpture of the Italian Renaissance. It would simply be the case that no more than a quantitative or metaphysical (and perhaps an epistemological) diminution would result. An emptiness would be created—a hole in space-becoming-time, a lacuna in process.

The same may be said of some narrative. For instance, *The Palm-Wine Drinkard* by Amos Tutuola is a collection of individually intriguing wonder tales held together in the frame of a man's continuing search of the underworld for his palm-wine tapster. These tales do not eventuate from one another. Each is discrete, existing in narrational frontality. They never compose into a whole. But as there are exceptions to the isolation of the syndetic array in sculpture, so is there also in narrative—though the instance I have in mind is a late work, reflecting a European influence, so that the work is eventuating and yet at the same time also syndetic. To perceive this better, I shall briefly consider the *Oba Waja,* a "tragic" opera by Duro Ladipo. Let me begin with the elementary observation that tragedy as such is not common in the Yoruba literary tradition; it is a borrowing. Yet because the opera's composer is profoundly Yoruba, we may expect the resultant acculturative work to bear the marks of both cultures.

I discovered in my earlier study of this work[12] that one may say that tragedy is such a form as forswears the mythoformal values at its substantive level—what it is *about*—while arighting them at a structural level. This is to say that the violated mythoform works inevitably toward its arighting. Thus, I argue, in the classic Greek world it was mythoformally the case that terms existed in opposition and that the inevitable movement—of life, of truth, of art—was toward their resolution. The mythoform was, in brief, synthetic in the *Oedipus Rex.* The tragic state was to be found in the fact that in Oedipus, that synthetic dynamic had gone awry, and this awryness is insisted in several ways: Oedipus, who is foot-wounded, must destroy the sphinx who is equally monstrous of foot. The Sphinx, further, is the product of an incestuous relationship between her mother, Echidna, and Echidna's offspring, Orthus, the dog. The theme of incest as a wrongness of synthesis, is made theme and variation of the play, and throughout is to be seen as an energy—a power—of the play. That the proper eventuation of things should be thwarted is the deep cause for tragic concern, and that they should be arighted and their error expiated is reason for deep joy.

In Yorubaland, where it is not synthesis but syndesis which rules, the case is otherwise. Upon his lord's death, the commander of horse is required to commit suicide in order (syndetically) to accompany his king into heaven. That he fails to do so is a refusal of the syndetic imperative. But the mythoform will, and does, prevail. The commander's son returns home and, finding the family's obligation unfulfilled, slays himself, as fitting and due sacrifice to augment the king's entry into heaven. Syndetism pervades the work in its presentation: music augments words, dance augments song. The chorus sings praise names, litanous recitations of the virtues of an individual, syndetically enacting his power for all who hear. I should also remark the syndetism of format: the nineteen-page script is broken into five acts! Even allowing for the fact that as opera the elapsed time for each act will

---

12. See my "Tragedy—Greek and Yoruba."

be greater than this fact would suggest, yet an average of less than four pages per act argues strong interest in density of event.

Finally, let me remark the interesting fact that the actors stand over-whelmingly in address not to each other but to the audience. *Oba Waja* is not primarily an interactive play. This feature is to be seen as the literary similetic equivalent of that frontality I have noted in the works of sculptural array.

The Yoruba aesthetic is a syndetic one, not solely in the fact that in both the aesthetic of invocation and in the aesthetic of vituosity it proceeds through syndesis, but also in the sense that in order to achieve fullness the one is posited upon the other. We see further evidence of this in the range of variations possible in joining homomorphy of substance or of form with a complementary heteromorphy thereof. One suspects that obscurely there exists at base some significant system of the relationships of homomorphy and heteromorphy, one suggested also in the odds and evens of numerology as well as in the earlier Gelede and ibeji analysis. This would clearly be consistent with the imperative toward syndetism, stemming from the myth-oform. Surely the addition of homomorphy to heteromorphy constitutes a further, and perhaps consummate, achievement of heteromorphy wherein, one suspects, the most gratifying enactment of Yoruba syndetism is to be found.

In the range and complexity of their exploitation of the conceivable sorts of syndesis and continuity, the Yoruba seem to be distinguished from other peoples of Africa. We perceive that the Yoruba derive a deep joy from the mythoform's repetition of itself.

The Yoruba mythoform as seen in sculpture—and one presumes the case would be little different if one turned his attentions to any of the other arts—is thus to be understood as comprised in part of specifically Yoruba dynamics (wide syndetic exploitation of sculptural arrays, a complementary aesthetic holding in complementary balance aspects that are both invocative and virtuosic); in part of Pan-African elements; and in further part of phases that occur broadly among the ancient, nonindustrial cultures of man and seem to constitute elemental terms for the enactment of affecting presence. Meanwhile, also to be seen in Yoruba works writ in the entirety of corpus, there also exist such marked stylistic variables that, for example, very differ-ent interpretations of the general characteristics of "ibeji-ness" are to be encountered (see plates 23–25). There can be no doubt that between the poles of the most general and the most particular there exist critical questions with respect to determining those points, precisely, at which one defines the mythoform. The concept of the mythoform is, thus, "a tool lightly to be held in hand." Although the mythoform of the Yoruba as I have described it cannot "generate" the precise conditions of all the Yoruba substyles of ibejis, it can nonetheless "generate" the general conditions of those styles—those respects in which "Yoruba ibeji-ness" is to be defined, those very terms which, despite local visual and volumetric variations, permit any experienced viewer of Yoruba sculpture to identify given works as ibeji. Although at present I do not know the nature of the terms to be employed, I know that at some future point I shall be able to articulate the meaningful respects in which *Yoruba,* for example, is to be found in works. These terms will be so distinctive that they will both distinguish Yoruba works from the works of all neighboring peoples and also override such stylistic particularities as are to be found from town to town. With respect to the broadly African and broadly human conditions of the Yoruba mythoform, it is doubtful that these variously discernible phases are to be viewed as having increasingly "deep" powers that variably inform the work. Rather, for the present at least, we must doubtless view them solely as coequal (if not historically coeval) constituents.

Although it is possible, given our limited understanding of the complexities of the human consciousness, that the more general levels are in fact more deeply and more powerfully rooted in consciousness, we still have no way to ascertain whether these variably deep conditions are of distinctive existential consequences. We do know that this configuration of mythoformal phases, executed in a work, constitutes the necessary and sufficient conditions under which the Yoruba consciousness may be made incarnate as presence within a work.

THE POWERS OF
THE MYTHOFORM II

We have seen that the Yoruba mythoform is a particularity of emphasis and of richness of mix respecting the syndetic; it is of a special modulation of continuity such that it is frequently achieved atomistically (or pointillistically) and is to be seen as an act of subordinating continuity to syndesis; and it displays a singularity of style within these special emphases—never precisely to be duplicated by any other people—which makes the works distinctively Yoruba. With respect to intension, Yoruba works are not significantly distinguishable from those of most other black African cultures.

We have seen that these general dynamics are, in one respect or another, common among "tribal" peoples the world over (all continents and significant—i.e., culturally particular—islands), and we can conclude from this broad distribution that such dynamics are ancient conditions under which the human consciousness is made to stand in apperception of the world. Indeed, each of them, together with their alternatives (synthesis, discontinuity, extension) is to be considered mythologemic—although their cultural selection, weighting, and interpretation are mythoformal.

How ancient these dynamics are we do not yet know. But I think we must reconsider the adjective "ancient" and substitute for it "primal," in that the very dynamic of syndetic intensive continuity we observe in Yoruba and other "tribal" traditions can be shown (at least syndesis and intension can) to be the systemic energy of the earliest works of affecting presence produced by man—dating from 30,000 to 10,000 years ago, during the European Upper Paleolithic period.

So, it is erroneous to think of the deep caves of the Franco-Cantabrian area, those vaults inhabited by man's most ancient paintings, as no more than tombs filled with the cultural detritus of Upper Paleolithic man-kind—a kind of aesthetic kitchenmidden. The forms of animals (and of a few manlike creatures) there painted, or modeled, or graven upon floors, walls, and ceilings—though they be decaying—are still alive. For the life of a work of affecting presence lies in its ability to compel, and these robustly sinuous works are perhaps as compelling as any works of affecting presence available to mankind.

Because they still own presence, these works can hardly be said to be a kind of ancient artifacture—of interest, yet somehow mute because divorced from those ancient peoples in whose consciousness their "mean-ings" were to be found. No, these works remain as real to us today as they were to those peoples several hundred centuries ago. If we no longer know *all* their aspects of being as they originally were, in those times for which they were made, yet we can know some; for that consciousness which they enacted then they enact still, and it abides a residual power within each of us.

Thus, if their *meaning* is lost to us, their *being* is not. Those ancient publics were doubtless as aware as we of the powerful presence that there abides. Not tombs, these caves, but eloquent though wordless theatres of the enacting consciousness of millennia past, abiding out of the epoch of their begetting, reaching out to quicken our own consciousness today. Each work, for however long its colors or conformations will endure, will be the living of that very configuration of vital awareness, value, and affect with which it was initially informed. These works are not so much "remains" as they are visitors from ancient men. Their study is not so much archaeologi-cal—which I take to be the descriptive study of forms in their usages and chronological sequences—as it is "archaeidetic," which is to say of ancient consciousnesses.

This is not to suggest that archaeology is irrelevant to the study of these ancient works. Indeed, an understanding of their execution, their place in time, and the physical existence of their creators is of unquestionable value. But these works—or any works of affecting presence—are not ade-quately to be studied sub specie artifacture. What chiefly distinguishes them from the stone tools with which they shared history are two considerations: that they are as burdened with affect as with dimension, conformation, and color; and that their purposes are, today at least, esoteric rather than plain. That which is more than physical requires for its study that we take into consideration those special sorts of human action which such works are—

not residues, but incarnations of human consciousness and value. In order to entertain any notion of such inquiry, we must realize that as the perceptions of our own cultural heritage tend to make us *ethnocentric* in our understanding of cultures of our own day that are alien to us, so does our imprisonment in our own time cause us to be *chronocentric* with respect to the works of peoples of other times. Different times are different cultures. Still we can in some measure escape both of these centrisms. We are likely to be skewed in our understanding, to the extent that we permit ourselves to search for particularities of use, function, or "meaning." To the extent that we are as general as possible, we are, correspondingly, the more likely to be both safe and correct. Therefore if we look at these figured works as direct and immediate presentations of the very mythoforms of consciousness, we can then come to see them not merely as pictures but as living apprehensions of the world. We can let these ancient forms themselves *in-form* us as to the enduring vitality of that archaic consciousness they incarnate even into this latter day, and which still abides in us.

The universality of both the systematic nature of consciousness (in terms of which it tends to enact common energies in multifarious ways) and the pervasion of the human consciousness by the aesthetic both conspire to suggest the notion that the cave art concerned the powerful—perhaps to such a degree that we might think of it as sacral. This in turn inclines us toward the belief that the obscure figure in the cave of Trois Frères we have come to call "the Sorcerer" (plate 77) is in fact a being immanent with power, an explicit excresence, a personification of the powerful energies that inform the caves. The Sorcerer is either a man *masked* as a deer and gloved with the paws of another animal, or else he is a composite being: part deer, part bear, part man. Whatever the particularity of his raison d'être, we may never be able to say. Yet we can state that he is an enactment of those primal persuasions that constitution is through addition, and that this yields incrementation, which is an enactment of power.

The Sorcerer is not the only instance of syndetism at Trois Frères, nor, indeed, in the other caves as well. One of the chief mysteries of cave art is to be found in our ancestors' relatively commonplace habit of superimposing figures, so that several figures might successively be rendered upon the same surface. This is so remarkable a kind of action—in that it could hardly have served to advance clarity of the perception of the works—that underlying the practice must have been a reason deriving from the urgencies of the enacting consciousness. Because the witnessing of the works was thus down-played, one can only presume that what was important was not the perception of the acts so much as their commission. Further, we must conclude that the commission of the act in the particular place of superimposition was important, else clarity of rendition would not have been sacrificed. Thus, successive repetition of an act, or of kinds of acts, is a clear instance of the syndetic creation of power through supplementation. It is only the invocation of the dynamic of syndesis which can make any sense of so extraordinary a phenomenon.

The projectiles loosed against certain of the painted animals (or plants overpainted—it really makes no difference which) are further instances of syndesis (whether they had been painted as original or subsequently superimposed)—as are the dots painted or graven upon the flanks of some animals, and for that matter, the dots executed upon the surfaces of the caves and not within the contexts of any outlined animals (plate 78). The extraordinary rarity of works that could be called "compositions"— which one defines as works of multiple figures caused to exist *with respect to one another in clear or suggested relationships*—also suggests a drive toward a discreteness of act.

Indeed, in some sense one could argue that the "work" of Upper Paleolithic presence is in any given instance to be read as the wholeness of the cave; and its usages—including those processes by means of which that wholeness exists as the sum total of all its individual enactments—are to be regarded as visually, but not, perhaps, metaphysically, discrete. The caves are suffused with the power of the syndetic, and whatever else the paintings and sculptures and engravings might have been, they were also celebrations of the additive nature of things. Perhaps it is only this dynamic which can explain the presence therein, at one and the same time, of works surviving over a great span of time (about 20,000 years).

Syndetism not only predominates as a dynamic of consciousness among many of the world's peoples, it is also absent—one suspects—from none of them. Think, for example, of the abiding interest in games that characterizes our own culture. Gambling and sports are merely eventuations of syndetic actions of a limited sort whose various throws follow one another not by consequence but merely by sequence. Because syndetism is so pervasive, both synchronically and diachronically, it is reasonable to presume it an ancient property of the human consciousness. Conserved within us today, it reads its archaic evidences upon cave walls with a certain intimacy and familiarity. At minimum, therefore, we may assert that we see at work in the ancient cave arts of Europe the immemorial dynamic of asserting power through increase, and of effecting increase through accretion.

There is, in the second place, another fact we must bear in mind. The Upper Paleolithic seems to have been pervaded by a marked stylistic homogeneity. Paolo Graziosi speaks to this:

> In certain essential respects Franco-Cantabrian Palaeolithic art has a fundamental unity from its inception to its conclusion, notwithstanding the changes in subject matter, technique, conception and, probably, purpose, that it underwent in the course of time. We can therefore speak, in a general sense, of a definite aesthetic concept in Franco-Cantabrian art as a whole, when we wish to follow its main lines of development.[1]

It is only by recognizing this aesthetic consistency that I can enjoy the latitude I must have to make the following argument, for I wish to adduce evidence from a consideration of works dispersed throughout the long period. The purpose in so doing is found in the opportunity to call attention to some particularly strong conformational themes that characterize the spatiality of works from the periods under consideration, themes we may also take to be basal terms under which the consciousness itself enacts the lived world of the epoch.

I choose as my point of departure the various "Venus" figures whose characteristics tend to be generic, which is to say that certain features are common among the figures under consideration. These are: a careful coiffure, featureless face, polysarcic masses of breasts, heavy abdomens, and vast legs which rapidly attenuate into feetless points (plate 79). These figures are exaggerations of the female form, and some observers are led to the notion that they are concerned with "fertility." But this represents an order of particularity we may not address. The most we can reasonably say of them is that it is fair to expect that during a period of glaciation, and given a diet rich in fats, the female body might be expected to store adipose tissues in the areas and of the quantities suggested by these stone figures.

In some cases, it is markedly ambiguous whether a form is that of a woman or of a phallus (plate 81), inasmuch as the stylized rendition of the neckless head and the ponderous breasts tend to be remarkably suggestive of the male genitalia. Yet the representation of the male body itself is rare.

1. Paolo Graziosi, *Palaeolithic Art,* p. 23.

When it is depicted, it tends to be much more summarily treated. But one point is clear: whether of female or of phallus, the forms enact a core. Indeed, if one accepts the point about "one aesthetic" for the Upper Paleolithic, one may observe that, differences in age notwithstanding, in silhouette the Venus figures remind one of no form so much as of the stone blade (plate 80). Each tapers toward points at its ends, and correspondingly each swells toward its middle. Now this is true most dramatically of the broader tools. However, narrow ones, such as gravers, are analogous—if less dramatic—with similar features of wider middles and attenuated ends. The frontal shapes of the narrower points actually remind one of the profiles of the broader tools. Indeed, in quite exaggerated form, one of the Venus figures tends to suggest the outline of a narrower point. This pervasion of the theme of the core we may call "coreality," intending thereby to suggest both *core-ality* and *core-reality*.

The figures achieve their emphatic rendition of the core not only through middle swelling and distal diminution, but also through a significant intension of the arms, usually folded across the body. But intension, though it may help in the achievement of coreality, is not to be confounded with it. To see this more clearly, it is useful to distinguish between lateral and vertical intension—the former an inhibition of the spatial extension of the body at flexed joints, and the latter a curtailment of exuberant or elaborate treatments of the head and feet. The people of the Upper Paleolithic nearly always exercised a clear penchant for both lateral and vertical intension, save in the case of the antlered animals, where there also appeared an interest in vertical extension. This is a difficult case to read, however, owing to the incredible size and complexity of the racks some antlered animals achieve.

The Venus figures enact not only coreality but also both lateral and vertical intension. So also do the bisons and the bulls painted upon the galleries' walls, especially so in the later art of the cave at Altamira in contrast with that of Lascaux. The bison is naturally coreal with its diminished hind quarters, its enormous shoulders, and the smallness of its face. Yet even so, its coreality appears to be emphasized in these parietal works. In the later work at Altamira, coreality is even more markedly emphasized by turning the head of the bison back upon its flank (plate 82).

We may, in fact, invoke this concept of coreality to explain the overwhelming interest in profilism in the cave paintings. The instances of full frontal view are rare, limited almost entirely to the treatment of the horns in some animals shown in twisted perspective (plate 82), the face of the Sorcerer, and a lioness (these quite nearly exhausting the inventory of such instances). We note that even among animals less "coreal" than bull and bison—the deer, the horse—the rendering of the work in profile permits the presentation in emphasis of the curved, coreal abdominal area of the animal. The so-called Chinese horse of Lascaux provides excellent evidence of such emphasis (plate 83).

The evidence from the Upper Paleolithic suggests that coreality is the primal spatial condition of the mythoformal consciousness of the period. Intension, although also evident in the works of the period, seems to be a dynamic exerted in the service of coreality. Extension does not appear to be a significant discipline. Its occurrence is limited to those elements that normally extend into space: antlers, the ears of a rabbit, the horns of a bull.

Because the consciousness is systematized, revealing in the common characteristics of things its own deep regularities, we may propose that coreality appears as primal to the human consciousness as syndetism. And, one may suggest, the concurrence of the two dynamics into syndetic coreality constituted the terms by means of which the Paleolithic consciousness invaded and construed the world, ordering it a lived-world as coreal in social and intellectual and spiritual life as in its works of affecting presence and in its technological extrusions into blades, scrapers, and hand axes.

The fact is that these works reach out to us with a drama which argues that the consciousness is subject not only to concordance but also to conservation. Thus if we recognize something familiar in the Sorcerer, it is because he is an entity graven as reconditely upon the walls of our most ancient being as upon the remote wall of Trois Frères. He is the genius of syndetism and the master of transformation—twice mythic! The Sorcerer is a profound fact within each of us, a living ancestor of our own consciousness poised in an instant of enactment, obscurely rich with significance we cannot precisely identify, for the retention of ancient dynamics does not imply the memory of ancient contents. What the Sorcerer presents to us is significance pure, as a dream does. Certainly it is significance primal, a significance that millennia later produced the minotaur, satyrs, the devil, and the horned masks and helmets of Africa, America, and Asia which enrich men through their accretion of the spirits of gods or of beasts.

We cannot precisely identify because we have lost specificity of memory, and because our history, growing through exponentially intensifying change, has brought to our present consciousness complexities that diffuse the energies originating in the deep centers of the Sorcerer-consciousness. Thus, the consciousness of cave-art man was simpler than ours, in the respect that it did not have buried within it those numerous subsequent developments to which we today are heir. The deepest sources of our own consciousness, where the creation of the human world arises, were perhaps uppermost with him. One achievement of the cave artists is clear: their primary creation appears to have been a dimension of the human consciousness itself, that which we call myth.

The Sorcerer lurks in each of us. At our hominid base we are all magicians, for we have created the world itself as we have created him, not of a unity that physical science or logic might discern, but of this and that: inconsistencies—feet and calves of man, paws of bear, face of deer. He is the Sorcerer of tropes, of the dynamic by means of which the human consciousness exists in the world. It is this ancient power of making through which we know him.

This notion of the conservation of consciousness is an old one, familiar to Freud and Jung, and forming much of the thought of our time. The history of the evolution of man's body seems repeated in the stages of the intrauterine life. So is the history of the rise and development of man's consciousness repeated—not embryologically, but in every beat of our being. We deeply live the consciousness of ancient man as surely as we do the recent consciousness of our unique, last moment passed. And we live the ancient and the present simultaneously. Because the primeval endures with the new, we experience that stereotemporality which makes the self-in-time three-dimensional—in *was, is,* and *shall-be.*

Yet the consciousness we retain of our primordial past filters through the lenses of our intervening present, the earlier always in terms of the later. A consequence of this is that we may tend to overrationalize phenomena of the past, "seeing" ourselves as making flint tools and weapons or as painting upon cave walls. We can look back upon that ancient consciousness— chronocentrically—but this protoconsciousness that abides within us is too undifferentiated to comprehend differentiations that lie subsequent to itself. However, in our dreams, in the universality of the phenomena of affecting presence, and in our animation of the world it looks forth upon us—often at the expense of that reason of which we are so vain.

In short, we "know" about the Sorcerer of Trois Frères more than our topmost minds can readily identify. We know that he is a *creation* (in that no being actually or organically like him exists—or ever did). We know that his appearance among all other kinds of works is exceptional. And we know that his creation was for a reason. That reason was probably social rather than idiosyncratic.

Thus, though we seem to be so far removed from the Sorcerer, and though we view through the prism of today that distant point of light in which he stands in the long spectrum between the protoconsciousness and the consciousness of today, yet do we recognize him. He is the equivalent in consciousness of the tool, designed to cope with the world of the immaterial in a fashion similar to that in which celts and projectile points extended man's efficacy in the world of the material. The Sorcerer was a means for managing that ancient causality which lay beyond the powers of man's stone artifacture. Yet we must remember that both the tools and what we call the "art" (and I here suggest that to a consciousness differently constituted from our own the two might have been the same) were technologies of stone (and, to some extent, bone)—the stone's being exploited in both instances primarily by taking advantage of natural conformations and by chipping into shape and by working in low relief. So is it that the Sorcerer is to be seen as of a wholeness with this stone consciousness.

That coreal consciousness of which the Sorcerer is a visual poem could be something of this sort: man apperceived the world as an environment of force—coming from the unknown and eventuating into the slightly known. The long stability of the consciousness during the Upper Paleolithic, as signified by the slow and minimal change during the long epoch, suggests an even slower period of change prior to that period. The possible result of this was that the reservoirs of consciousness during the Upper Paleolithic (or prior to then—*when* makes little difference, for I am speaking of the Upper Paleolithic mainly as a hypothetical state of the consciousness) were not as deep as they are today, with our long history between then and now.

The parietal works were effective in relating the self—in this life and perhaps after it as well—to force. Perhaps, further, the artifacture of the self enjoyed as great an order of probable success as the artifacture of the body used upon the world (the distinction perhaps defining one of the first fruits of the behavioral revolution and an intransigent determinant of all those revolutions that followed). One concludes that this success was sufficient, however, to cause man to hold on—for people did manage to survive, and survival implies a measure of effective success in both areas. I presume, for the purposes of this exercise in creative anthropology, that tools, weapons, and "art" at this time were all perceived in very much the same way. This is not of course to suggest that the obvious differences among things were not recognized, but rather that they were commonly apperceived as entitive pragmatics—tools incarnating power, power-causing tools. My argument of the conservation of consciousness permits me to cite as evidence of this commingled pragmatism and presence the animism with which man at various places and times has invested his weapons, his tools, his environment (the Kris in Java, the sword in medieval Europe, the ancestor figure in Africa, the mana-bearing rock in the Pacific).

As the stone and bone artifactures reveal a common virtuosity of dimensional conformation (the chipping of the points, the modeling by both pigment and surface in the cases of the parietal artifacts), so from the systematization of culture may we imagine that a similar kind of pragmative-affective "chipping and modeling" characterized the rest of existence as well—both language and social structure, for instance. And so we may imagine these cultural phenomena to have been a kind of coreal social artifactures: language (or languages) I would presume would have been minimal of declension, and close of conjugations, productive of blunt utterances for chipping away at the imponderables of existence, and withal less dedicated to articulating the individual wants and anxieties than the important tasks of coherence of the person to the group and of the group to the power-that-prevailed; social structure—small, coreal units based upon common blood.

To suggest that the Sorcerer of Trois Frères is to be apprehended as having a status in the world little different from that of the hand axe is not to minimize it. For it is easy to imagine that the hand axe might then have been quite differently apperceived at a time when so few kinds of implements were available to man, making the difference between his survival and his extinction. Thus it was an enactment of himself in his universe of force. The Sorcerer represents a specialization in the total universe of the forms of man's work, but even so the terms of that universe were not numerous, being limited to a few animals, a few anthromorphs, a few hand prints, and (much more rare) a few dots—perhaps symbolic, perhaps presentational . . . the uncloyed enactment of pure syndetism.

The Sorcerer is an organization of traits that do not occur together and can do so only through invention. Indeed, perhaps it was the act of joining the disparate traits that created power of sort, measure, and force sufficient to whatever task it addressed. The uniqueness of the work suggests that the purposes which lay behind its execution, whatever they may have been, were statistically of a different character or order from those which lay behind the execution of all those other forms which exist in multiple renditions in the caves.

There appear at this remove to be but two possibilities concerning the ontological status of the Sorcerer: either that he enacted, or that he alluded to a being. But if the consciousness of man then had been different from ours today, it is possible that in that estate there might have existed no distinction between these two conditions. In such a case, there may have been a consciousness not characterized by such a variety of categories, as of true and false, real and imaginary, but rather only by a core, faceted arduously to utility. The reason of system would lead us to believe that this dynamic would have been a process in the enactment of force, not merely brutish force, but also a generalized force of the nature of the orders of man's existence in the world—the consciousness of prevailing or yielding.

There is yet a further comment to be entered concerning the Sorcerer of Trois Frères: the situation presented by the fact that the other works of the caves enact factual entities while the Sorcerer enacts a fictive one reveals that man's behavioral revolution had spread to include the imaginal, and the consciousness of man was reconstrued, extending from the bounds of the natural into the boundlessness of the preternatural. If it awes us, as indeed it does, it is because—dumbly perhaps—in some atavistic way we recognize the power of this revelation, and our psyches do with it what they do with all such signal achievements in the definition of man: they convert to myth.

If we assent to the notion of a common point of departure for human consciousness, then the diversity found in the kinds of consciousness in human populations suggests that in addition to conservation, the human consciousness is characterized by plasticity. This plasticity is to be observed not only synchronically (diversity of culture implies diversity of consciousness, in that culture is the generalization of individual consciousness), but also diachronically. We may not presume that ancient man was, in the structural dynamic of his consciousness, naught else than modern man with a simple technology. The relationship between consciousness and culture is one of absolute parity, with culture either embodying (in works of affecting presence) or evidencing the mythoform. The consciousness must be of a sort to enact that which it has enacted. Material cultural remains, therefore, are indices to the begetting consciousness. The homogeneity of culture persuades that the soft parts of culture (performances, feelings, the textures of existence) were homologous to the hard parts.

As judged by the stone remains, we must assume the range of the Upper Paleolithic culture to have been restricted. Indeed, we may imagine that it was "nodulated" in a fashion identical to the consciousness of which it was an enactment, with little significant distinction between the sacred and the profane; and that the social structure was coextensive with both, and perhaps conceptually (to our ancestors) indistinguishable from the cultural business of feeding, propagation, and self-protection. The problems of existence were as given as stone. Like the stones, they defined an obdurate mass to be chipped away and given as effective a definition as possible. That core was doubtless of such a nature that it had two aspects: the unpredictable and the unknown. The Sorcerer of Trois Frères was thus a chip of certitude upon the edge of this monolithic void that constituted the unpredictable world of Upper Paleolithic man.

But one might at this point wish to know in what respects the Sorcerer might be understood differently to chip away at the massive, coreal void. Do not the presences of the other creatures that figure in his parietal contexts similarly enact that human consciousness I have been describing? In order to provide an answer, we must think of man's works as extensions of himself, enacting his own relationship of power with the world. In this context one sees that the parietal works perpetrated a new dimension of that power—and the increased ranging of his problems of existence might be inferred from this development. Now the other works upon those Upper Paleolithic surfaces show man's growing power relationship with the essences—in some sense—of the other creatures of the world. The great import of the Sorcerer is that it provides us with testimony to the fact that at that point he interjected himself into the world of figured essences, thus through projection demonstrating a control upon the self that he had previously demonstrated only upon the faunal context in which the self existed. Once the self was itself extended into the world, great promise accrued to man's ability to manage the world through his works. The fact that females, and male and female genitalia—all enacted in these sites—were similarly corporeal and corelike suggests they thus bear common import. Yet the Sorcerer seems to hold greater significance because it reveals man as seen under new auspices: as related to the rest of the animal world (or the rest of the animal world related to him); as connected with—and indeed, when we consider the Sorcerer's maker, as inventor of—that which is not given by nature; and as changeling.

The articulation of man's self as combinatory, through his sense of invention, of other kinds of animals was a most dramatic achievement. It must stand as a critical juncture in the evolution of human consciousness, just as did the painting of animals, and prior to that the discovery of how to manufacture tools and weapons.

But there exists an even greater breadth to the importance of the human discovery achieved in the Sorcerer of Trois Frères, for the diachronic and synchronic pervasiveness of the phenomenon of masking argues that the Sorcerer is in all probability less likely to be a composite creature per se than a *man-masked.* Perhaps after the discovery symbolized by the presence of the Sorcerer, man was able, so protected, to undertake the perilous journey into the center of the immaterial and unknown body of the void upon whose edges he lived. Surely the mask must rank alongside fire as one of man's most important discoveries—perhaps an even more important discovery in terms of his behavioral revolution. For the mask must be seen to have released man's psyche from its imprisonment in his givenness. Perhaps the apparent singularity of the Sorcerer in the corpus of Upper Paleolithic works is thus to be explained, for that which is revolutionary tends at first to be of singular nature.

The universe of the mythic is one of constant configurations of consciousness, for an apperception of the world once achieved becomes an option for all humans; these apperceptions help constitute systems in which the most archaic abides and most deeply moves our personal beings. Earlier consciousnesses project either through or upon subsequent ones. No neurological inquiry accounts for such rich and confounding subtlety. Although both Freud and Jung understood this principle of the conservation of the consciousness, the former was limited by tending to restrict the consciousness to the autobiographical, whereas the latter, perhaps, did not sufficiently distinguish among the powers of that turbulent, strong deep he had discovered.

Yet the archetypality (which is recurring mythic energy) of the Sorcerer cannot be made on the basis of primordiality alone. The paintings of the bisons are as old, yet they are not archetypal—not as bisons, at least. But if the bison is not archetypal, there is that which is mythic about it, accounting for the particular power of its presence. This mythic element is that which it enacts along with the Sorcerer: the energies of the core. In the case of the Sorcerer, this power of the core is syndetically joined to that of the power of transformation.

The archetypality of the core deserves a few remarks in passing. One must note the formal similarities between corporeal intension and the forms of the male and the female genitalia. Being freed from his sexual enslavement to periodicity so that he could engage in sexual intercourse at any time was doubtless one of man's most significant liberations. Its dramatic import was perhaps very great indeed and might well have dominated man's first sallies into external works, thus implicating the "core" as the dynamic of the primeval mythoform of artifacture.

Conservation of the myths of intensive coreality and of syndetic transformation can be demonstrated by more than just a profound "shock of recognition." These basal energies have prevailed in man, resurfacing from time to time in subsequent art histories. We have seen them among numerous of the world's "primitive" peoples; we note them in earlier European cultures; and we have seen that they reoccur at the present time in modern cultures.

Anthropologists usually attribute such similarities either to the processes of culture contact or to the operation of accident—the fortuitous settling upon similar forms. Quite clearly, the extraordinary identities with respect to the exploitation of coreality, intension, continuity, and syndetism over such vast areas of the world (and as removed from one another as Nigeria and New Guinea) are not satisfactorily explained by diffusion; or if by diffusion, then in history so ancient that it antedates the rise of those orchestrations of differences that produced different cultures. Nor does the principle of accident obtain. Instead, we are faced with the clear suggestion, it seems to me, of a principle of the human psyche, a term in the inventory of man's behavioral options guaranteed to him as a member of Homo sapiens.

In the preceding chapter we considered the first category of the prevalence of syndesis and intension. I shall now briefly comment upon the other two. First, in further demonstration of the atavism of the intensive and continuous syndetism, one thinks of its reemergence during the European Middle Ages. Consider the confinement of sculptured figures to tight spaces in the cathedrals, arms across breasts, or at side, or bearing hagiographic identifications. And recall the tight continuity given figures by the long folds of garments, and the rather characteristic elongation of figures and features. As for syndetism, one once again thinks the architectural donations of the figural elements themselves. Further, when the figures were freed from architectural service and instead were used to grace altars, one thinks to the fact that they were given sacrifices in the form of gifts, ornaments, real clothing, flowers, small medals, and the energies of the light of many candles.

Second, in our modern period, intension has been strongly reasserted in the works of Rodin, Brancusi, and Zuñiga—and coreality has been reaffirmed in the works of Barbara Hepworth and Henry Moore. Syndetism is, of course, one of the most significant rediscoveries of our time—in the various "-ages" of contemporary art: collage, decoupage, assemblage. Here, wholes are created out of bits and pieces, and each declarative with integrity, in classic enactments of syndetism, causing the energy of the whole to be created by the sheer weight of the totality of the parts, each part investing its own discrete particularity into the greater and transcendant wholeness.

We see already established in the arts of Upper Paleolithic man several nonverbal mythologems: the powerful place (the "sacred within," which I take the caves themselves to be); increase of power through the processes of accretion; assertion of the core; and the definition of the master of transformation. We also see there the pervasion of one dominant configuration of consciousness (intensive coreality), and, in addition, the apparent invention of the wholly imaginative. Indeed, one wonders whether one might not think of the figuration itself (mimesis—correspondence with the world) as of the nature of a mythologem, one which has held for over 30,000 years.

The painters of the Upper Paleolithic apprehended self and world in some of the same mythologemic and mythformal energies we encounter today, yet they owned (as the Yoruba artists do) their own formulation thereof. That emphasis the Yoruba lavish upon syndesis, those most ancient of our ancestors devoted to that special version of intension I have called "coreality." And the power of the mask to transform was as known to them as it is to us, as was the power of place. Indeed, perhaps the Sorcerer at Trois Frères is as ancestral to the dancers of Gelede, and the caves of the Franco-Cantabrian as ancestral to the Yorubas' sacred groves and kingly palaces as those men and women are to men and women today. Certainly the primal nature of this syndetic-intension endows these dynamics with both primacy and the authenticity of originary usages. Certainly also those common consciousnesses between them and us bridge the millennia, most miraculously. And also certainly their availability to us today proves that a power of consciousness once formulated becomes a resource for all the successive generations of humankind.

6 THE POWERS OF CELEBRATION

The work of affecting presence exists as a point in the purposeful confluences of various subjectivizing powers: (1) metaphysical, involving the belief in the transferability of essences; (2) epistemic, deriving from the historical accumulation of values not directly demonstrable as present physical properties of a work—for example, the fact that of two works one might be revered more greatly than another, though to objective judgment they might appear indistinguishable, or not sufficiently distinguishable to account for their differences; (3) formal, textural, and other physical properties culturally held to be the necessary conditions for the existence of a member of whatever kind of work a piece is held to be; (4) mythologemic; (5) mythoformal; and (6) analogic facticity, the power of the made-thing. These are all powers of cognition—of apperception rather than of perception—and they are of the diaconsciousness; they inform the work with *depth* of subjectivity.

The diachronic energies illuminate the work into presence in either primary or secondary ways. *Primary* works present the mythoformal and the mythologemic forthrightly (as Tar Baby incarnates the theme of additivity, or as Oedipus does mal-synthesis, being the husband of his mother). In the Olowe bowl, intension and syndesis are neither mere allusions within the work, nor are they obscure. They are compelling and unmixed, in mythoformal purity generating deep portions of the work's apperceptual and virtuosic powers. In the instance of Gelede masks, in addition to their intensive syndesis, the items own as well—and fundamentally—powerful mythologems of earth goddesses and witches. The mythic is given as such.

Secondary works, in contrast, are those in which the mythic tends to hide rather than to stand forthrightly in its purity—to be the point of departure for the work's particularities rather than its uncloyed substance. Thus, in a photograph of Queen Victoria and her brood, the mythologem of motherhood—so powerful in the Pieta (and in the Anyi figure, plate 9) —becomes submerged in biographical particularities. Ardent particularity is inhospitable to prime presence. And the enactment of the mythoformal at the expense of the mythologemic defines that condition in which, in addition to serious works, the decorative is to be found. If the particularity of the work—its recognizability—tends toward the dilution of the mythologemic, by so much will that work hunger after mightiness of presence.

This attenuated, lessened secondary mythologemic illumination of a work is a function of its particular identifiability of either the work's content or the consciousness-of in which the content is subjectivized in the work. The mythologemic is timeless and of the diaconscious, but its lessening into secondary illumination is a function of particularization; it is *not* of the diaconscious.

The work as a point is forever encountered discretely in time and space. It is witnessed in an encounter of the synconscious. The synconscious names the seventh power of the work of affecting presence—that of the particularity of both its "subject matter" and its apprehension. For the work is seldom mythologem pure, but rather a particularity thereof—a given ancestor or maternity figure, a special eventuation, and so on. Further, as to the particularity of apprehension, an ineluctable condition of the work's power is the magnitude of its reception by its witness, for a work of affecting presence can no more than a human person strike its witness with greater power than that witness's sensitivities will permit. Encounter is ever in the synconscious, whose structure is of great and subtle complexity. It is only in the rich configurations of the synconsciousness that the diaconsciousness is knowable to us.

The name of the existence of the work in all the powers of its presence is "celebration," which is the establishment of the subjectivized thing in the seminal richnesses of diaconscious depth *and* in the familiarities of the synchronic consciousness. It is called "celebrative" because in the work, the powers of consciousness are enacted not simply in order to stand *as* awarenesses of the world and the self, but rather to cause them and to perpetuate them in their own analogic terms and for their own sake. The diachronic and synchronic conditions of consciousness are celebrated in the work irrespective of whether the aesthetic be of invocation or of virtuosity, for in either case the work is at base invoked into being—whether through the invocation of blood in sacrifice, the presence of a god, or the mighty stirrings of virtuosity.

My determination that no responsible or reliable theory of the aesthetic can exist without an adequate theory concerning the nature of the consciousness of which the aesthetic is an estate cannot be realized solely upon the diaconsciousness. I must also provide some indication of the nature of the synchronic consciousness in which the work of affecting presence is encountered in its particularity.

The consciousness is not only general and impersonal. The photographic film is "general," too—and "impersonal" as well. It is characterized universally with the same "mythic" power, that of making what is not a photograph become a photograph. Yet it can become a photograph only by becoming particular: it must have its generality "translated" into the specificity of what, finally, we perceive it to be. Imaging is the sole power of the film; and imaging lies inherent in every such image we see. It is so also with the consciousness. Whether it does so either in general terms (i.e., in terms known to all men [mythologems], or in terms particularly known to the culture [mythoforms], or in both) or in terms so particular that the mythopoetic is an obscurely troubling presence of innominate power, the consciousness enacts what it is within it to enact. Thus the powers of the consciousness exist either drawn like tides by mighty gravities of the moons of the mythic, gaining import and mystery and growing in great potency for our individual lives; or they retain their autobiographical idiopoeticity, as intimations, vague or acute, that augment our moments of the present; or, finally, they are explicit, as memories.

Consciousness is rather like the sea: at particular depths creating particular pressures and having characteristic life forms, these relating as a system into formidable deeps, attenuating upward. This sea is at once both the whole inscrutable evolution of mankind and is all men. But at the same time each human wholly surrounds and contains it. Our lives are its vast, irregular shores, its countless plains, and its trenches whose bottoms none can ever know. We are, each of us, ever aheave with the deep swellings and drawings of tides, the forces of the psychically viscuous amnios of our being. But the deeps own their surface. However molded by their mighty tides and swellings, they are at their tops subject also to the whimsies of the present sun and the momentary winds. The topmost domain of the waves is the world of the synconsciousness. Here the waters of the deeps thrust, subject to the restlessness of particularities of conformation and force.

The synconsciousness is not, of course, specificities themselves, but the ability of the consciousness to specify. It is where the particular happens. No animal, I suspect, has so richly embraced the particularity of things as has man. Other animals seem to live life as a narrow given. It is difficult to imagine the fly has any particularity to the frog; it is, one suspects, rather but of the generality of food. Man alone seems freed from the absolute tyranny of the general, pursuing specifics not for the sake of mere existence but for the virtuosities of their delights. Inasmuch as the human surface is a tension atop the deeps, man may at any moment in his specificities feel the loomings of the general. Thus an offending object might in an instant become no longer merely a hammer that strikes a thumb, but obdurate and malevolent: an animate will that wishes us pain, so that we curse it. Upon such a brief instantaneity and for that space of time alone the hammer is imbued with presence moving toward the existence (though not achieving the status) of a work of affecting presence.

The deeps do not recall the plenitudes of waves, but the waves reveal the presence of the deeps. The recognition of the identities of waves is the power of particularity. This is the action of the *indicative* mode. (N.B. The fact that I use grammatical terms for some of these modes should be taken as an acknowledgment that—however imperfectly—language is, after all, an attempt to structure the system of our *reportage upon* and our *verbal construction* of the world so that it might have some degree of conformity to the system of our being.) The indicative is the mode of our passive and recognizing reception of the world. Here the world rests in its utter quiddity, silently existing in a state of culturally given oughtness, fixed in culturally defined space as surely as in culturally defined time, construed as to the dynamics of the mythoform and by discrete particles of explanatory tales which serve to validate both the terms of the world's and our existence and also the possibilities of its usages and our own.

The experience of the consciousness is, like the sea, undulant, and before one swelling of it retires, the successive one is awake. The instant the world of the indicative is or must be subjected to alteration, the sense of the givenness of things is suspended—unless that change be part of the pattern of the rightness of the existence of things, as in the movement from systole to diastole. There is no givenness to the *kind* of change that then occurs; it can be into one or more of five other modes of the synconsciousness. If it is directed toward efficacies, it is *pragmative;* if the estate is wrong or insufficient, it may be *imperatively* arighted, or caused to be; or the world may be reconstrued according to a divinely inspired order or by virtue of a divine suspension of the mundane, in which event the consciousness comes to be construed after the mode of the *subjunctive*. The perceived orders of the world may be transferred from the world itself to the interior of man's thinking about them; then perceptions of quiddities are displaced by conceptual essences, and these swell into awarenesses addressed and arranged in viable estates they may or may not have in the indicative world. Such is the mode of the *cerebrative* (or *conceptual*). Finally, the quiddities of the world may be infused with an indwelling of man's awareness of them, so that they are given in a state of being-held-in-consciousness-of. This is, of course, the mode of the *celebrative*. Whereas in the indicative, the mythologemic and the mythoformal abide passive, in all the other modes they are active, in each mode according to the special nature thereof. It is important to recognize that as the analogic cannot be equivalently enacted in the digital (no matter how we describe a ball, we can never constitute it in words or numbers), so also the apperception or enactment of the world according to one mode cannot be equivalently apperceived or enacted in any other mode; thus the celebrative can never be enacted in the cerebrative. This is true notwithstanding the fact that multimodal apperception or enactment of a given phenomenon can be achieved, with the result that we bring about that strange, epiphenomenal echoing quality of the world of lived ambiguities that is our existence.

In the *pragmative,* the mythopoeia of the world is made operational, according to (1) universal principles (e.g., mechanics; the pragmatival equivalent of the mythologemic), and (2) cultural principles (e.g., a figurehead sculpted as the bowsprit of a ship; a face carved upon a heddle pulley among the Baoule of the Ivory Coast; a fetish, held to be adequate to the control of the powers others might have over one). The pragmative mode is one which changes items or states into instrumental objects and processes, whether these be words (a recipe), forces (a siphon), work arms (levers), substances (foods, chemicals, wood, fire), or whatever.

Whether in an injunction respecting one's personal conduct in his society, or in the institution and maintenance of states, the *imperative* exists in a sense of the obligatoriness of things (e.g., "Thou shalt not . . ."). In both the pragmative and the imperative, one coerces the world. But whereas in the pragmative one coerces the world instrumentally, in the imperative one does so compulsively, through moral, intellectual, or spiritual urgencies. In the imperative, the world and man are brought to a state of rightness. It is conceivable under multimodality that one could imperatively enact the pragmative, as when a king honors a pledge to God by building a cathedral.

The subjunctive is the actualization of the mode of "what-if-it-were?"—where the boundaries between self and other, this and that, natural and supernatural cease to exist and where *that which was not—and could not be—is.* Where *that which could not be* comes into being, *that which can easily be* is displaced. The subjunctive is the mode of mystical transport and possession at one end of the subjunctival spectrum, and at the other mere legerdemain. The voices of the subjunctive are glossolalia and prophecy on the one hand, the fairy tale somewhere in between, and the lexical con games of the advertising industry on the other (soap will make the ugly beautiful and deodorant will render the smelly acceptable).

Under the aegis of the cerebrative the objects and events of the world are displaced by insubstantial and mentalistic abstractions by means of which one constitutes an immaterial world, complete with relations which may be either simple or complex and which are either existent in the external world or are wholly imaginary. One can also build through its symbols certain analogic creations of human experiences: of meaning in an essay, of complex relationships among conceptual elements in philosophy and science. This inner universe of orders and powers embraces the mathematical as well as the semantic, and the relationships among imaginary bits (as in astrology) as readily as those among real bits (as in astronomy).

But of all the modes, the celebrative is of greatest interest to us. Like the subjunctive—and some may argue the mathematical construct as well—the celebrative is the mode of presence. But in the subjunctive, the subjectivity established is of a human or divine self with human body locus, whereas in the celebrative the subjectivity established is located within a work and is, unlike the veritable person, forever limited to but one apperception. And in the cerebrative, if it be the case that the externalized thought is incarnated in subjectivity, then that subjectivity is neither in celebration of the mythic nor is it conceived and perpetuated in affect. Its characteristic is not value but truth.

"Celebrative" is the recognition (in our uppermost consciousness—in our *knowing*—and in a condition of affect) of the fact that there exists in the work an intransitivity of presence. This intransitivity results from the fact that the work exists in its own presence. There is in the work no sense of the creator's using the work but as a "language"—a "medium" in which he "writes" a "message" extrinsic to the work itself. This would be a transitive state of affairs. Being intransitive, the work retains rather than refers its constellated powers. It is this self-sufficiency of the work which causes it to be *celebrative.*

Yet there is more than this. In the other modes of the consciousness, the deep energies of the analogic and the mythic are task-directed. But in the celebrative they are invoked for their own sake. Thus intension, syndetism, and continuity—from work to work—each (or in the instance of the Olowe bowl, *all*) becomes a theme in the work's presence, to be repeated over and over, this way and that. These repetitions serve not functional ends in the same sense that a tool or a formula does, but rather serve forthrightly and im-mediately to celebrate the conditions of the possibility of a Yoruba consciousness of the world.

The nature of the celebrative never became more clear than in the last several decades of American painting. Here space, color, conformation, semblance, substance—all have traditionally been part of the item or the work of affecting presence, bent toward the service of enacting "content," by which I mean to denominate socially agreed points in the self's or the world's recognizabilities, the *mimetic.* But mimesis is only one option toward affecting presence; it is merely a kind of ethnocentricity of culture, time, or reason, one which causes us to ask, concerning an unfamiliar work, "What *is* it? What does it mean?"

But recent artists have abandoned the mimetic, releasing color, conformation, and the other resources from servitude to the well-known and easy "contents" of depiction, narration, and the like. This liberation comes about in recognition of the fact that light itself can bear the affect of the consciousness' subjectivity, as can color, conformation, all of them. Shorn of the burdens of representation, of their dependence upon the familiarities of the objects and events of the world, these im-media, in the purity of their nonmimetic presentation, now exhibit those "in-their-own-terms" and "for-their-own-sake" powers of autonomy, which are the hallmark of the celebrative.

One need only look at much of the work done during these two decades to see this great escape. Barbara Hepworth uses volume toward its own ends; she enacts filled space, not mimesis. Albers does not use color toward the ends of coloring the things of the world; he employs its properties toward their own presentational ends so that they become analogic estates of consciousness-of in their own terms. And Stella uses conformation not as a property of something else, but as its own thing. Oldenberg employs semblance to deobjectify the object, as Rauschenberg bends scraps of content toward "content-less"—or perhaps supercontent—ends. Similar movements occur in the other arts, where sequences and time, tones and prolongations are created not for the purposes of tonal depiction (melody) but for those of pure presentation. For more than 30,000 years we have experimented with celebration-as-content. How revolutionary the aesthetic of pure im-mediation might ultimately prove to be, only the next 300 centuries might show.

Where the existence of the aesthetic lies in power rather than in perception, the nonmimetic employments of the affecting im-media are more to be expected than wondered at. Whereas a portrait or a landscape is at base a semblance, there is no similar sense of imitation in the work of invocation. Power pure—power actual, not virtual—is the analogic achievement of invocation. The pure consciousness-bearing of an Albers color field is the virtuosic counterpart of the power which infuses the whiteness of kaolin with which Yorubas cover their bodies on certain occasions; and the mound of earth for Eshu is shape-bearing homage. Shape and color, thus, are used im-mediately, for their specific presentational ends and not for the ends of semblance. This is the significance of the celebrative. (Of course, what I say here must not be taken to mean that at the level of synchronic particularity there is not a sense of celebrating far less esoteric, and indeed even mimetic powers. Ibeji celebrate the particularity of twins as well as the power of doubling; Egungun masks celebrate a generic portraiture as well as the triumph of the invocation of the ancestors.)

The various modes of the synconsciousness are amenable to combinations, one with the other, and so each may exist in the field of the celebrative, as each may exist in the fields of the pragmative, and so on. Indeed, one may grid these possible combinations, as I do here (figure 3), solely to sort out the classes of the analogic that may be discerned from culture to culture. I shall provide a rough gloss of the celebrative and its intersections, using various Yoruba works toward that end.

The Yoruba invoked work is a *Gesamtkunstwerk*, syndetically compiling into a fullness objects, occasion, donations (metaphysical, epistemic, and physical), verbal creations, and—often—music and dance. The *work* thus achieved is nonmimetic, though the items (e.g., the mask) may be, establishing no recognizable thing in the world save itself. The Yoruba *Gesamtkunstwerk* is thus abstract, of the category of the purely celebrative (ambit of the farthest right in the grid). In its primary invocation of mythologem and

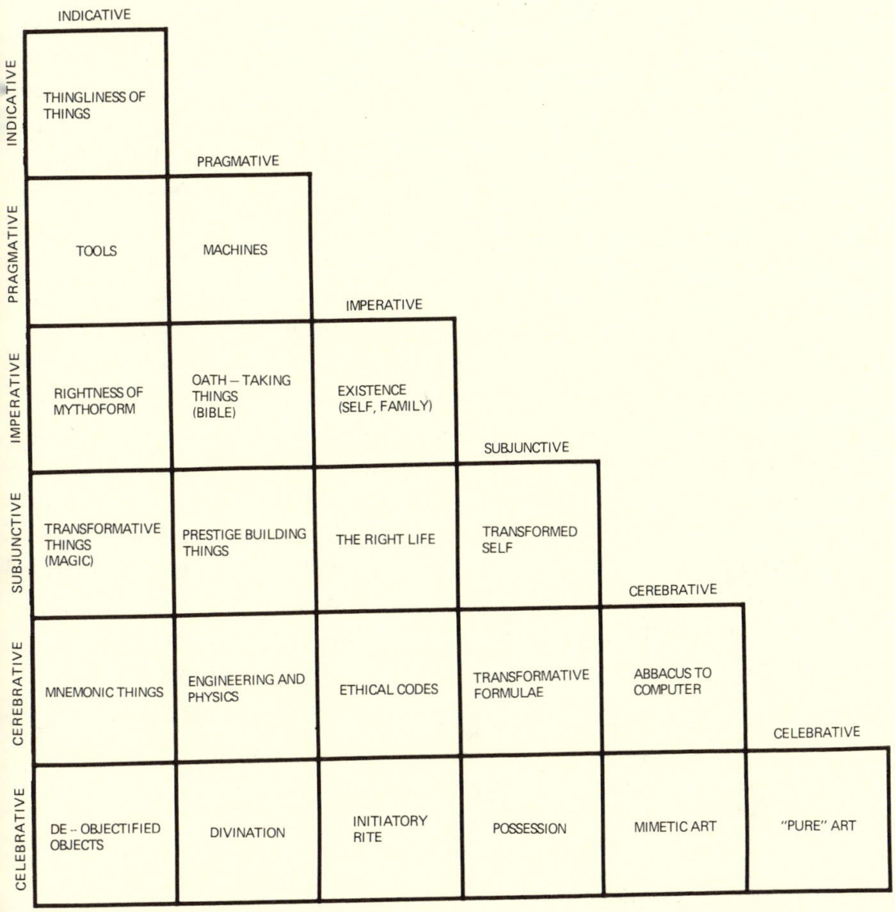

	INDICATIVE	PRAGMATIVE	IMPERATIVE	SUBJUNCTIVE	CEREBRATIVE	CELEBRATIVE
INDICATIVE	THINGLINESS OF THINGS					
PRAGMATIVE	TOOLS	MACHINES				
IMPERATIVE	RIGHTNESS OF MYTHOFORM	OATH – TAKING THINGS (BIBLE)	EXISTENCE (SELF, FAMILY)			
SUBJUNCTIVE	TRANSFORMATIVE THINGS (MAGIC)	PRESTIGE BUILDING THINGS	THE RIGHT LIFE	TRANSFORMED SELF		
CEREBRATIVE	MNEMONIC THINGS	ENGINEERING AND PHYSICS	ETHICAL CODES	TRANSFORMATIVE FORMULAE	ABBACUS TO COMPUTER	
CELEBRATIVE	DE – OBJECTIFIED OBJECTS	DIVINATION	INITIATORY RITE	POSSESSION	MIMETIC ART	"PURE" ART

THE MODES OF THE SYNCONSCIOUSNESS

Figure 3.

mythoform it celebrates the conditions of Yoruba consciousness, monu-mentalizing those primal energies of being-conscious by virtue of intransi-tively enacting them in the work. In the Gelede ceremony, for example, syndesis enacts itself toward the end of defeating the antisyndesis of infer-tility.

Mimesis (taking the next ambit) tends to occur among the work's items. Thus, although the drumming of the Gelede ceremony is mimetic of naught (being enactive in a straightforward fashion of the Yoruba processes of dynamic, space, and time), the dance steps of the paired female-masked dancers, with intricate precision synaesthetically enacting the drumbeat, are mimetic—of the drumming itself. There are other instances of mimesis in items as well: ibeji are "fed" actual food; the bases of the Gelede masks are mimetic of a beautiful Yoruba face; the ibeji's beads and scars lend them a certain personal identity; and so on.

The ambit labelled "subjunctive celebrative" is intended to acknowledge that in relationship between work and witness, the witness exists in the act of being transformed *by* work. The difference between the double subjunctive (see figure 3, when the subjunctive intersects itself) and the subjunctive celebrative lies precisely here. The former is the transformed self, the latter is the work in the power of causing the displacement of the diurnal self and its transmutation into the powerful or divine.

I think of no Yoruba piece as importantly associated with the initiation of young men into the secret lore of their people as some of the bush-spirit masks so common among the peoples of the Ivory Coast, Liberia, Sierra Leone, and Guinea. Jacqueline Delange writes of such masks among the Toma people who live in the border areas between Sierra Leone and Ivory Coast:

> In the region which at the beginning of our century was jokingly called the "Liberian Tyrol" live the Toma. . . . Behind the last huts of the villages, the dense forest permits the occurrence of initiations, shelters the instruments of the rituals, and easily conceals the secrets of the more or less archaic institutions. A large mask made of heavy wood calls the young into the forest and returns them to the village after the month of initiation.[1]

The young men enter the bush pawns of the inscrutable and terrible powers of the mask; but they leave the bush having been brought into new life, understanding the esoteric doctrines which previously had been denied them.

The "pragmative celebrative" is exampled by divination, which in the case of the Yoruba is particularly apt. The process of divination is conducted under the invocation of both Ifa (who knows the will of the Creator God Olorun) and Eshu (who presides over the uncertainties of life). These are *presences,* not mere allusions, and the successive and discrete cast-

1. Jacqueline Delange, *The Art and Peoples of Black Africa,* p. 50.

ings of the divining beads syndetically enact the autobiographical estate of the person on behalf of whom the divination has been undertaken.

Any work which moves from noninvoked to invoked, as a mask often does, moves from objectness to deobjectivization, so that item invoked into work bears to item as object a relation similar to that which obtains between a humdrum icebag and the celebration of the absurdity of "icebag-ness" when its size is greatly magnified and subsequently installed in a museum gallery.

Each of the modes of the synconsciousness involves a difference in the uses of the energies of apperception. Yet as between any two modes there exist areas where energies of both sorts are simultaneously operative—brought to focus, illuminating our beings and the world with complex acts of apperception. The indicative tends to be tinged with a strong sense of oughtness characteristic of the imperative; righteousness can be entailed in the subjunctive; or there may be a sense of displacement about the cerebrative. It is only rarely (as in the art-for-art movement) that we try to adhere to, and to find excellence in, purity of categoreal apperception. When modal purity is sought, intermodal ambiguity is correspondingly diminished. It is for this additional reason that it is wrong, for instance, to search for "meaning" (which is of the mode of the cerebrative) in the work of contemporary idiopoetic art, for the movement toward modal purity has accelerated to such an extent that familiarity of either theme or conformation has systematically been eliminated. (Obviously this is true of some art only—minimal, conceptual, abstract; it is clearly not true of photorealism.) Even the virtuosities themselves in such cases become subject to a new virtuosity, namely that of the violation of virtuosity, so that mere excellence might no more stand in the way of the achievement of the work than "content" once did.

Unlike the powers of the diaconsciousness—where the power of facticity is more primal than the mythologemic, and where the mythologemic is antecedent to the mythoformal—the powers of the synconsciousness do not exist in a hierarchy of evolutionary order. This is the case even though the modes of the synconsciousness did not all come into existence at once but were variously and separately achieved in the aeons of human evolution. Yet with respect to one another, these modes of consciousness may be said to exist in a kind of order when considered in terms of the points they occupy upon the continuum that stretches between objectivity (being object) and subjectivity (being subject). The order seems to be as follows: indicative, pragmatic, cerebrative, imperative, subjunctive, and celebrative. In this listing the indicative is the most objective, and the celebrative the most subjective. It is critical to note, however, that only the indicative mode is wholly of objects as given. All the others are more or less rooted in—but take their points of departure as extrapolations from—the given world of indicative objectivity.

One may also describe order with respect to the consideration of the continuum concerning the explicit givenness as opposed to the explicit causability of the world. In the indicative mode, the world is most given and least explicitly causable. By "explicitly causable," I mean causable by virtue of the action in a given mode of the individual upon the world. The world's givenness is comprised chiefly of the indicative mode; its causability (beyond simple, pragmative causability) of the five remaining modes, in each of which the world is equally but wholly differently causable.

Each of the modes of causability rests upon a different premise concerning the causability of the world, as follows:

MODE	*PREMISE*
Pragmative	The world is manipulable. (the use of the world, as well as its goodness, is maximizable)
Cerebrative	The world is conceivable. (causable through concept)
Imperative	The nature of man is perfectible. (causable through fiat)
Subjunctive	The self of man can infuse the world; the self of god can infuse both world and man. (causable through transfiguration)
Celebrative	The world is enrichable through man's subjectivizing enactment of it. (causable through presentation)

In each of these modes the premise is active, existing only in the mode's enactment of the world. The premise is the set, the tenor, the believed presentness of the consciousness in the mode or modes of any instant of apprehension which constitute its present duration. It is the auspices under which the engaged psyche is existent. Indeed, it is perhaps most useful to think of the premise of a mode of consciousness as its *key*, in the musical sense of that term. It is desirable to use the term "key," because it offers the strategic advantage of connoting a qualitative and analogic modal particularity whose principle of variability is existential and whose variations are as from intellective to affective to imperatival states, for instance, rather than from one kind of conceptuality to another. "Key" is also a useful image for the further advantage it offers us in coming to an understanding of *how* it is that tHe myth informs the modes, which is to say as a common melody may inform a musical execution in successively different keys. Within a given key all perception that occurs is of a modal sameness, and the being established within a key is unique to that existential set which it is. It is important further to stress that although any of the modes may provide the key signature for any stretch of engagement of the consciousness, in point of fact it is more likely the case that the actual living of life is overwhelmingly characterized by the simultaneity of engagement of the consciousness in several—or indeed even in *all*—of the modal keys. So in the fabric of living is the world both given and caused, and the latter, in each of the five modes of causability. So is a roundedness, a wholeness, given to the dynamic of our engagement with the world.

The individual is a uniqueness through the prism of whose existence, in every instant of his own time, the deep powers of the mythologemic and the mythoformal are refracted into the specificities of the synconsciousness. It is not that this mythopoetic realm is a remote, Platonic ideal. It is in each of us the indwelling power of the possibility of our conscious being, the imprinting energy of all we do and can conceivably do. It is the power of our being mammalian, Homo sapiens, cultural, and individual. It is as specific in causing us to be men, as is that in bees which causes bees to be bees, and is not one whit more—or less—mystical. So the mythopoetic power of analogicity eventuates into the power of things; the mythopoetic powers of the mythologemic and the mythoformal incarnate the analogic, subjectivizing it into works of affecting presence. These powers are also codified in laws; they inform the articulation of the procedures of our science; they are portentous of things to come; they reach splendors and mightinesses in affecting presence; and they guide us in our manipulation of those items of the world they have identified for us and have charged with their own significance.

The energies of the mythic are general and find their strongest incarnations in works that greatly enact the general. For this reason it is in those cultures with highly socialized forms of affecting presence that the mythopoetic tends most clearly to be omnipresent. Where, in contrast, human pursuit is always directed toward the most particular and the novel, the power of the mythic tends to appear diminished, sometimes to such an extent that it is difficult to see how it abides even in the least, endowing a work with the presence of history and the concerns of mankind. It is the generality of the mythic which, in cultures enacting an aesthetic of the power of invocation, brings about the syndetic exploitation of multiplicities of the modes of the synconsciousness. This intermodal syndesis is to be seen in all works of invocation. The general requires the sacrifice of particularities. In an aesthetic of virtuosity, in contrast, the movement is toward the highly focused and away from the syndetic (save insofar as these are atavistically retained in poetry—where rhyme, rhythm, images, etc., successively enrich the work—or forthrightly exploited in such isolated movements as collage and assemblage).

If in the work of affecting presence the power of the diaconsciousness comes about by virtue of the fact that the work incarnates the general conditions under which man—as a mammal, a member of Homo sapiens, and a cultural being—enjoys consciousness, then the power of the synconsciousness derives from the work's incarnation of specificity. This is to say that unless—as in *Oedipus* and *Oba Waja* and Tar Baby and Galatea—the mythologemic and the mythoformal eventuate into dynamics and become personified in "actors" and in thematic "plots," then the work celebrates the mythic in terms of something other than the mythic itself. It becomes secondary rather than primary. The mythic is the pregnant radiance suffusing a work as a power of import; the synchronic is its faceted brilliance. The single act of apprehension which unitively enacts the diaconsciousness in terms of the synconsciousness throws each apperception—each instant of consciousness—into that fullness of dimensionality which endows it with the sense of *being-lived*.

The powers of the synconsciousness are the powers of the present, whereas those of the diaconsciousness are of the pulsing lineages of presence. Both are powers of apperception. At the point of intersection of these powers, presence exists, incarnated into the subjective analogic by virtue of being held in consciousness-of. This they do in the fullness of the awe man holds for the *thing,* in the infusion of thing with the primordial and general energies of the mythologems, in the cultural and historical determinants of the space-time-process in which the world is construed, and in the work's eloquence of present time and circumstance. The synconsciousness is made to stand upon the firm ground of the diaconsciousness, the transient idiopoetic upon the eternal mythopoetic. Mythologem is posited upon thing, as is mythoform; and mythologem upon mythologem; and mythoform thereupon; and (in tribal works or in truly great works of the aesthetic of virtuosity) all this is posited upon the discrete, its edges blurred however with the soft, diffusing radiances of the general.

The work of affecting presence may stand more toward the diachronic and mythopoetic—as do Yoruba works of invocation, and strongly mythicized works of our own time and place (e.g., Lipschitz's *Prometheus* and Melville's *Moby Dick*)—or more toward the synchronic. The work of affecting presence, whichever stream it emphasizes, is a whirling convection of energies, each stream an estate of consciousness, and each line of force related to each of the others. These linked constellations of consciousness swirl into vortex, and the witness drowns therein (possession in a culture of the aesthetic of invocation, that magnificent estate of aesthetic overload before a work of mighty virtuosity). These are those existential floods of consciousness-of which are the work's power in presence.

The work exists as presence and end in itself. This is owing to the fact that those relationships which by its nature the raw analogic enacts (social in relating individuals in power to others; efficacious in relating man through tools to the universe, so as to make its obdurate intractabilities amenable to the ends his body and mind require) are in the work of affecting presence not transferred—they do not stand as agencies in psychic transactions—but are *self-*contained.

The power of bodily analogic acts (kinesic, paralinguistic) lies in interrelating persons, and that of the factitious analogic lies in relating man in efficacy to the world in such a way that his physical (and many of his social) needs are satisfied. The unique power of the work-as-subject lies in the establishment of this entelechy, such that the interiority of self (whether as individual or as social group) is given the reality of existence within the world rather than simply within the individual.

The work of affecting presence is an activity of consciousness; it is either of the self apprehending the world in self's own terms, or it is of the world apprehending the self in the world's own terms. The former is a humanistic aesthetic, and usually tends to be of virtuosity, whereas the latter is ordinarily an aesthetic of gods and spirits, holding man in fee; it may be of either invocation or virtuosity. We shall truly come to "understand" something of the nature of the work of affecting presence when we realize that it is not a thing as such but a nexus of forces of consciousness-being-expended—yet never diminished thereby. It is awarenesses of the world and not color patterns that configure in Van Gogh's wheat field. There are colors to be sure, but they are more than the colors of the palette (for to regard them so is reductivistic); they are estates of the intention of the world.

Naturally, it is only the witness who can both perceive and apperceive the work; but it is only the work which can forever enact the same estate of standing in consciousness-of whatever it is that it intends. The colors of a painting do not *signify* or *symbolize* the intention of the sunflower; they are the viable conditions of that intention. The colors are not a language, they do not mediate the wheat field's perception; they are im-mediative of it, causing it to be.

It is this perpetrated and perpetuated consciousness which is the cause of the presence of the work; it is the work's endurance in it which is its activity; and it is the engagement of both in the mythologemic roots of being human—and in the mythoformal ones of being cultural—that establishes the power of the work. This is the process of *holding in self-consciousness.* It is the general class of which that phenomenon—which in poetry we call "metaphor"—is a special subset of instances.

The powers of the work of affecting presence are the powers of *being* subject. And the work is a subject because it exists in that estate of intending something which is a capability alone of a sentient being. Yet that work is also a subject because it has the power to execute itself as a subjective estate of being upon its witness.

The witnessing of the work of affecting presence is rooted in the fact of our being human. It rises through the orders of thingliness, through the mythologemic and the mythoformal—through which in great measure it asserts its subjectivity—to its efflorescence in the particularity of the syn-consciousness, where it completes its establishment as subject. If the experience of the work is often profound, it is so due to the great depth and breadth of lineage and enrichment which make the act of witnessing one of enormous complexity and vitality.

Only when we realize all this shall we be in that advantageous position from which we may inaugurate *appropriate* inquiry into the realms of the aesthetic and, correspondingly, enrich our understanding of Homo sapiens.

BIBLIOGRAPHY

Armstrong, Robert Plant. 1970. *Forms and Processes of African Sculpture.* Occasional Publication, no. 1. African and Afro-American Research Institute, Texas.

————. 1971. *The Affecting Presence: An Essay in Humanistic Anthropology.* Urbana: University of Illinois Press.

————. 1975. *Wellspring: On the Myth and Source of Culture.* Berkeley: The University of California Press.

————. 1976. "Tragedy—Greek and Yoruba: A Cross-Cultural Perspective." *Research in African Literatures,* no. 1, vol. 7, pp. 23–43.

Bateson, Gregory. 1972. *Steps to an Ecology of Mind.* New York: Ballantine.

Count, Earl W. 1973. *Being and Becoming Human: Essays on the Biogram.* New York: Van Nostrand Reinhold.

Crane, Hart. 1975. "Voyages." In *The Norton Anthology of Poetry,* rev. ed., edited by Alexander W. Allison et al., p. 1083. New York: W. Norton.

Delange, Jacqueline. 1974. *The Art and Peoples of Black Africa.* New York: E. P. Dutton.

Drewal, Henry John. 1975. "Gelede Masquerade: Imagery and Motif." *African Arts,* no. 4, vol. 7, pp. 8–19, 62–63.

Drewal, Margaret Thompson, and Drewal, Henry John. 1975. "Gelede Dance of the Western Yoruba." *African Arts,* no. 2, vol. 8, pp. 36–45.

Glassie, Henry. 1977. "Meaningful Things and Appropriate Myths: The Artifact's Place in American Studies." In *Prospects: An Annual of American Cultural Studies,* vol. 3, edited by Jack Salzman, pp. 1–49. New York: Burt Franklin.

Graziosi, Paolo. 1960. *Palaeolithic Art.* New York: McGraw-Hill.

Harper, Peggy. 1970. "The Role of Dance in the Gelede Ceremonies of the Village of Ijio," pp. 67–94. *Odu,* n.s., no. 4., Ife and Oxford.

Houlberg, Marilyn Hammersely. 1973. "Ibeji Images of the Yoruba." *African Arts,* no. 1, vol. 7, pp. 20–29.

Malevich, Kasimir. 1964. "Suprematism." In *Modern Artists on Art,* edited by Robert L. Herbert, pp. 92–102. Englewood Cliffs, N.J.: Prentice-Hall.

Ojo, G. J. Afolabi. 1966. *Yoruba Palaces: A Study of Afins of Yorubaland.* London: University of London.

Bibliography

Pemberton, John. 1975. "Eshu-Elegba: The Yoruba Trickster God." *African Arts,* no. 1, vol. 9, pp. 20–27, 66–70.

Thompson, Robert Farris. 1971. "Sons of Thunder: Twin Images Among the Oyo and Other Yoruba Groups." *African Arts,* no. 3, vol. 4, pp. 8–13, 77–80.

———. 1972. *Black Gods and Kings: Yoruba Art at UCLA.* Occasional Papers of the Museum and Laboratories of Ethnic Arts and Technology, no. 2.

———. 1978. *The Grand Detroit N'Kondi.* Bulletin of the Detroit Institute of Arts, no. 4, vol. 56.

Wimsatt, W. K., and Beardsley, Monroe C. 1971. "The Affective Fallacy," and "The Intentional Fallacy." In *Critical Theory since Plato,* edited by Hazard Adams, pp. 1022–31, and 1015–22. New York: Harcourt Brace Jovanovich.

Wright, David A. 1979. "An Analysis of Criticism concerning the Abstract Expressionist Paintings of Mark Rothko." Unpublished thesis, University of Texas at Dallas.

INDEX

1. Dogon mask, surmounted by an ancestor figure. (Private Collection)

2. Kongo oath-taking figure. A repository of accreted powers, invested with living oaths bound with the driven spikes. (Courtesy of the Detroit Institute of Arts, the African Art Fund)

3. A Yoruba ceremonial bowl, carved by the famous Olowe of Ise. (Courtesy of William Moore)

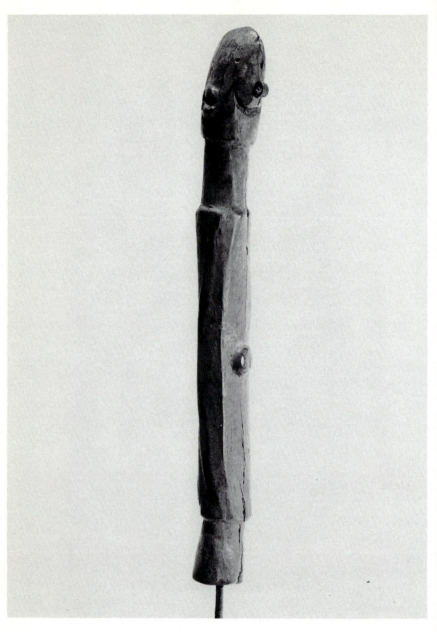

4. Waja figure. Note the absolute avoidance of lateral extension. (Courtesy of Shango Galleries, Dallas)

5. Yoruba Gelede mask. This and the following three Gelede headmasks own a class similarity, as to both function and appearance. (Private Collection)

6. Yoruba Gelede mask. (Private Collection)

7. Yoruba Gelede mask. (Private Collection)

8. Yoruba Gelede mask. (Courtesy of the Toledo Museum of Art; Gift of Edward Drummond Libbey)

9. Anyi maternity figure. (Private Collection)

9a. Anyi maternity figure, detail of hand, showing a degree of digital articulation uncommon in African sculptures. (Private Collection)

10. Yoruba Shango baton. Such batons are carried in processions honoring the god of thunder. Note the principle of twoness in the blades—carried on the right shoulder in plate 10, and surmounting the head in each of the others. (Robert Plant Armstrong)

11. Yoruba Shango baton. (Courtesy of the Harrison Eiteljorg Collection of African Art)

12. Yoruba Shango baton. (Courtesy of Harriet and Bryce Alpern, Detroit)

13. Yoruba Shango baton. (Private Collection)

14. Yoruba Shango baton. (Courtesy of the Paul and Ruth Tishman Collection)

15. Yoruba Egungun mask, worn in honor of ancestors. The masked wearer becomes infused with the ancestral presence. (Collection of the Art Institute of Chicago)

16. Yoruba Egungun mask. (Courtesy of Melvin and Iris Silverman)

17. Yoruba baton in honor of Eshu, the god presiding over indeterminacy. (Courtesy of Anne R. Whipple)

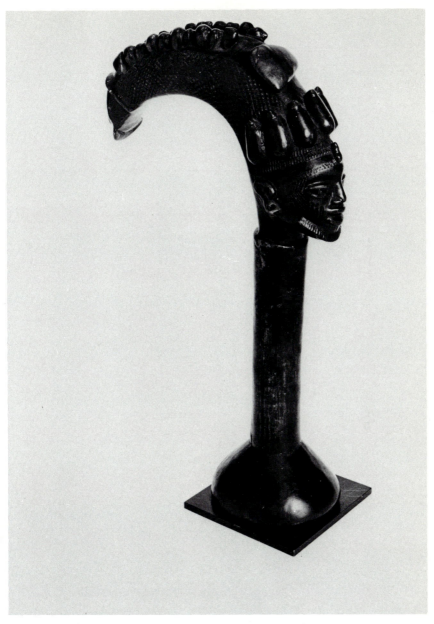

18. Yoruba Eshu baton. A twofold accretion of meanings lurks in the long cap, for its length is intended also to connote the phallus. (Private Collection)

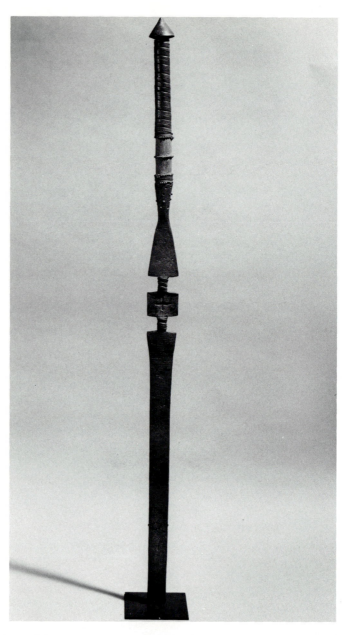

19. Yoruba staff for Oko, the agricultural deity. (Courtesy of the Pace Gallery, New York)

20. Staff for Osanyin, the Yoruba herbalist god. (Robert Plant Armstrong)

21. Yoruba divination tray, Ifa. The god of divination is the god of determinacy, the complement of Eshu (see plates 17, 18). (Courtesy of the Michael Oliver Gallery, New York)

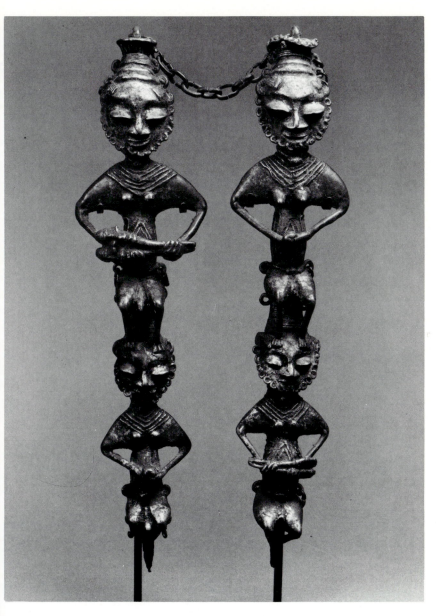

22. Brass figures (Edan) for a member of the Yoruba Ogboni society. Like the Ifa tray, these figures communicate divine knowledge to men, e.g., in this case of identifying witches. (Private Collection)

23. Yoruba twin figures. Twins are more common among the Yoruba than among any other human population. These figures, repositories of twins' spirits, are solicitously cared for since twins are capricious. (Courtesy of Mr. and Mrs. Donald F. Morris, Detroit)

24. Yoruba twin figures. (Courtesy of Mr. and Mrs. Donald F. Morris, Detroit)

25. Yoruba twin figures. (Private Collection)

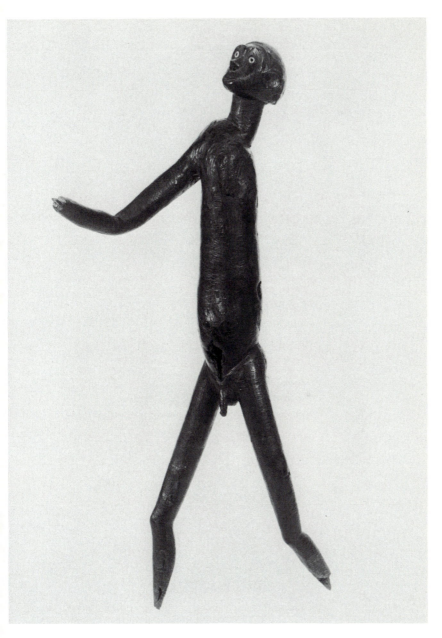

26. Wanyamwesi figure. This carving is executed in a degree of lateral extension unusual in African sculpture. (Private Collection)

27. Ashanti Akwaba figure. This figure's arms also show lateral extension, but it is minimal, not exceeding the head's diameter. (Courtesy of Charles Benenson)

28. Bassa figure. Minimal extension in the frontal plane. (Courtesy of Mr. and Mrs. Philip Sanfield)

29. Baoule ancestor figure. Note the scrupulous intension of the work. (Bequest of Victor K. Kiam, New York. Courtesy of the New Orleans Museum of Art)

30. Yoruba offertory bowl. Frontal extension is prevented by having the extended arms surround the bowl. (Courtesy of the Hammer Collection)

31. Chokwe figure. Note the exaggerations of hands and feet. (Kimbell Art Museum, Fort Worth. Photograph by Bob Wharton)

32. Basongye Kifwebe mask. This mask and the next four plates, representing works from widely separated places, reveal a common concern with facial lines. (Courtesy of Mr. and Mrs. Donald F. Morris, Detroit)

33. Bacham night mask. (Courtesy of the Detroit Institute of Arts, Eleanor Clay Ford Fund for African Art)

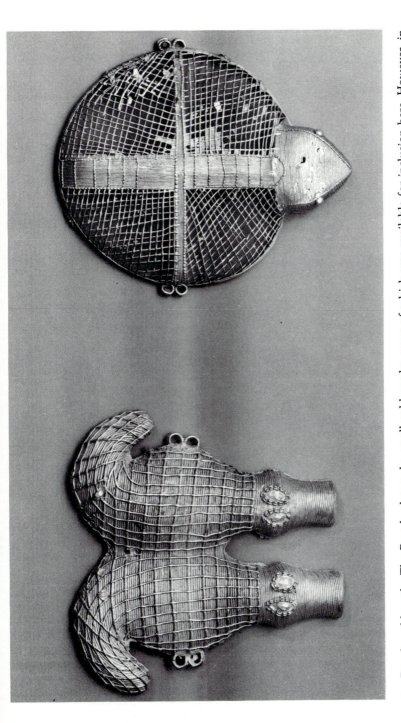

34. Baoule gold turtle. The Baoule also make small gold masks, none of which was available for inclusion here. However, in the face of such a mask, the theme "facial lines" is given a "technological" treatment similar to that seen on the turtle. (The Metropolitan Museum of Art, The Michael O. Rockefeller Memorial Collection of Primitive Art. Bequest of Nelson A. Rockefeller, 1979. All rights reserved, The Metropolitan Museum of Art)

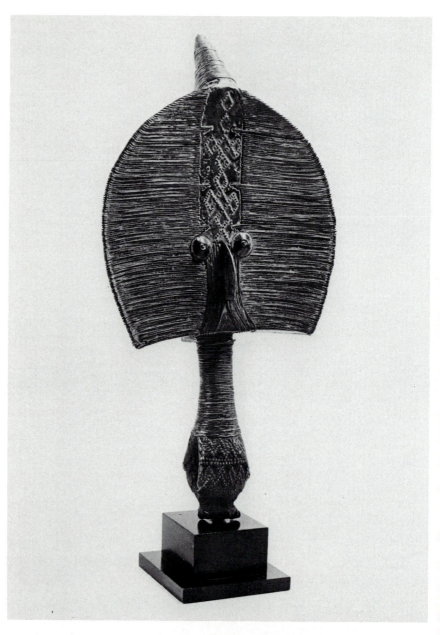

35. Hongwe figure. As in the Boule example, the facial lines here also result from a process of making. (Courtesy of Mr. and Mrs. Stanley Marcus)

35a. Hongwe figure. (Private Collection)

36. Dan mask. Among the Bambara there exists a "lion" mask whose face is covered with a single system of congruent facial lines. However, this piece was not available for publication. Accordingly, we use this example, which, while not fully lined, does show the trait in western distribution. (Courtesy of the Davis Gallery, New Orleans)

37. Mende figure. This and the next eight plates illustrate various interpretations and applications of the ringed-neck mythologem in African sculpture. Whereas here the rings are "fat," in other cases—e.g., the Benin head—they are conceived to be necklaces. (Private Collection)

37a. Mende figure (rear view). (Private Collection)

38. Benin head. (Courtesy of the Indiana University Art Museum)

39. Bissagos figure. (Private Collection)

40. Ebrie figure. (Courtesy of Mr. and Mrs. Philip Sanfield)

41. Basongye figure. (Courtesy of the Harry A. Franklin Family Collection, on loan to the Los Angeles County Museum of Art)

42. Basongye figure. (Courtesy of the Pace Gallery, New York)

43. Kuyu head. (Courtesy of Mr. and Mrs. William W. Brill)

44. Dengese figure. (The Metropolitan Museum of Art, The Michael O. Rockefeller Memorial Collection of Primitive Art. Gift of Nelson A. Rockefeller, *1969*. All rights reserved, The Metropolitan Museum of Art)

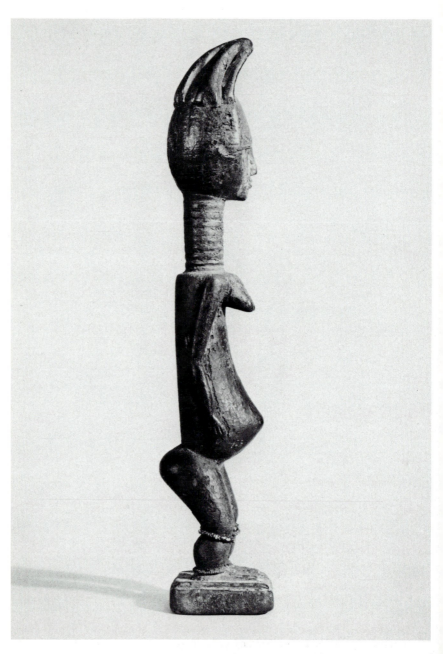

45. Anyi figure. (Courtesy of Roy and Sophia Sieber, Bloomington, Indiana)

46. Mumuye figure. Zig-zag or diamond-shaped legs are another in the inventory of plastic myths commonly encountered in African sculptures. The next five plates show treatments of this myth. (Robert Plant Armstrong)

47. Turka figure. (Courtesy of Mr. and Mrs. Brian Leyden)

48. Kaka figure. (The Metropolitan Museum of Art, Fletcher Fund, 1972. All rights
reserved, The Metropolitan Museum of Art)

49. Afo figure. (Courtesy of Melvin and Iris Silverman)

50. Lega figure. (The Metropolitan Museum of Art, The Michael O. Rockefeller
Memorial Collection of Primitive Art. Gift of Mr. and Mrs. Raymond Wielgus, 1967.
All rights reserved, The Metropolitan Museum of Art)

51. Boma figure. (Courtesy of the Dallas Museum of Fine Arts, The Clark and Francis Stillman Collection of Congo Sculpture. Gift of Eugene and Margaret McDermott)

52. Montol figure. A unitary pectoral-shoulder mass, often subject to dramatic
stylization, is one of the items in the inventory of African plastic myths. See also
plate 53. (Robert Plant Armstrong)

53. Senufo rhythm pounder. Unitary shoulder-pectoral mass. (Courtesy of the Dallas Museum of Fine Arts, The Gustave and Franyo Schindler Collection of African Sculpture. Gift of the McDermott Foundation in Honor of Eugene McDermott)

54. Fang figure. A marked forward-pitch of the shoulders is an African sculptural
mythologem. Perhaps this is a dynamic motif, reenacting a common African dance
movement. See also plate 55. (The Metropolitan Museum of Art, The Michael O.
Rockefeller Memorial Collection of Primitive Art. Bequest of Nelson A. Rockefeller,
1979. All rights reserved, The Metropolitan Museum of Art)

55. Mbole figure. (Courtesy of the Dallas Museum of Fine Arts, The Clark and Francis Stillman Collection of Congo Sculpture. Gift of Eugene and Margaret McDermott)

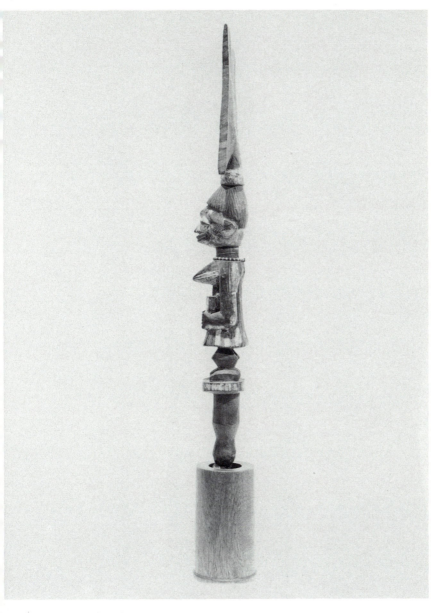

56. Yoruba Shango baton. In addition to various works already illustrated, which the text references document on this point, this baton dramatically enacts a rare instance of Yoruba use of zig-zag legs. (Robert Plant Armstrong)

57. Yoruba Epa mask. These masks (see also plates 58 and 59) may be either relatively simple or most complex. Note how the hands are executed as always *holding,* never free. (Robert Plant Armstrong)

58. Yoruba Epa mask. (Courtesy of the Toledo Museum of Art; Gift of Edward Drummond Libbey)

59. Yoruba Epa mask. (Courtesy of Melvin and Iris Silverman)

59a. Yoruba Epa mask (side view). (Courtesy of Melvin and Iris Silverman)

60. Yoruba crown. Beads are a medium ideally suited to the achievement of an effect dear to the Yoruba—atomistic continuity, an expression of syndesis. (Courtesy of the Minneapolis Institute of Arts)

61. Fang figure. Note the monochromatic surface. (Courtesy of the Pace Gallery, New York)

62. Yoruba bowl. Surfacial homomorphy. (Courtesy of the Michael Oliver Gallery, New York)

63. Yoruba Magbo mask. Surfacial heteromorphy. (Courtesy of the Harrison Eiteljorg Collection of African Art)

63a. Yoruba Magbo mask (¾ view). (Courtesy of the Harrison Eiteljorg Collection of African Art)

64. Yoruba crown. Formal vertical homomorphy. (Courtesy of the Indianapolis Museum of Art, Emma Harter Sweetser Fund)

66. Yoruba figure. Formal vertical heteromorphy. (Courtesy of the Pace Gallery,
New York.)

67. Yoruba Edan rods. Formal ventral heteromorphy. (Robert Plant Armstrong)

68. Yoruba divination board. Formal radial heteromorphy. (Courtesy of the Hammer Collection)

69. Yoruba housepost. Substantive vertical homomorphy. (Courtesy of Richard and Jan Baum, Los Angeles)

70. Yoruba bowl. Substantive ventral homomorphy. (Private Collection)

71. Yoruba housepost. Substantive vertical heteromorphy. (Courtesy of Mr. and Mrs. George Schwelinger)

72. Yoruba axe. Substantive ventral heteromorphy. (Courtesy of the Pace Gallery, New York)

73. Yoruba stool. Substantive radial heteromorphy. (Robert Plant Armstrong)

74. Baoule maternity figure. (Courtesy of the New Orleans Museum of Art)

75. Fon brass group. (Courtesy of David and Barbara Ames)

76. Yoruba figure with bowl. Note unusual side-turned face. (Courtesy of Mort and Rebecca Lipkin)

77. The "sorcerer" of Trois Frères. Drawn illustrations by Sue Llewellyn, except for plate 80, which is drawn by Barbara Imber. The "sorcerer" is after Breuil.

78. Upper Paleolithic sign.

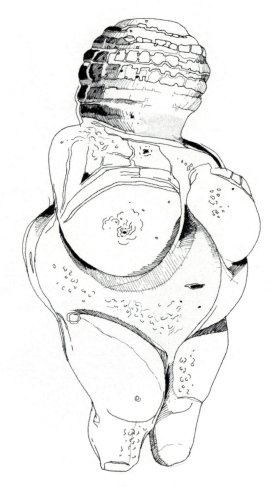

79. Upper Paleolithic "Venus."

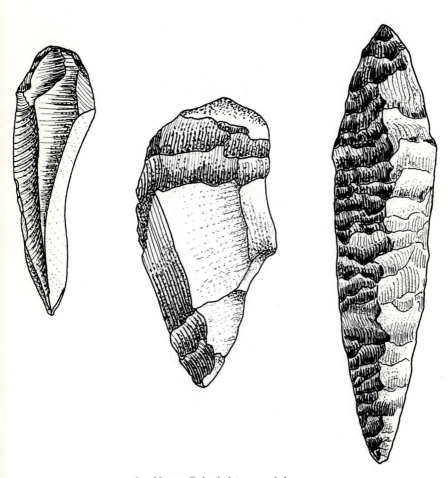

80. Upper Paleolithic coreal forms.

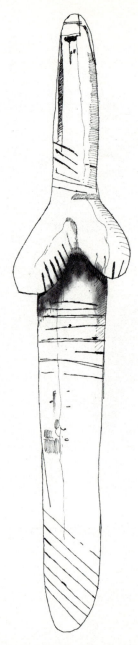

81. Upper Paleolithic "Venus."

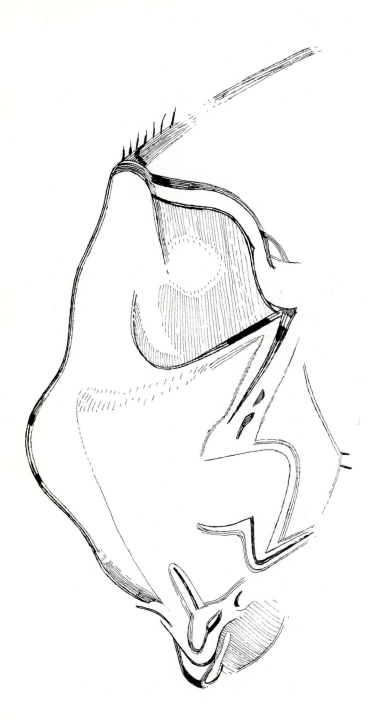

82. Upper Paleolithic bison.

83. Upper Paleolithic horse.